WonderFull

Ancient Psalms Ever New

Marty Machowski

Illustrated by Andy McGuire

New Growth Press, Greensboro, NC 27401
Text Copyright © 2020 by Marty Machowski.
Illustration Copyright © 2020 by Andy MacGuire. All rights reserved.
Published 2020.

Unless otherwise noted, Scripture quotations are from The Holy Bible, English Standard Version® (ESV®), copyright © 2001 by Crossway, a publishing ministry of Good News Publishers.

Scripture quotations marked (NIV) are taken from THE HOLY BIBLE, NEW INTERNATIONAL VERSION®, NIV ® Copyright © 1973, 1978, 1984, 2011 by Biblica, Inc.® Used by permission. All rights reserved worldwide.

Cover art: Andy McGuire
Interior art: Andy McGuire
Interior Design and Typesetting: Trish Mahoney

ISBN: 978-1-948130-74-5

Library of Congress Cataloging-in-Publication Data
Names: Machowski, Martin, 1963- author. | McGuire, Andy, (Illustrator)
   illustrator.
Title: Wonderfull : ancient Psalms ever new / Marty Machowski ; illustrated
   by Andy McGuire.
Description: Greensboro, NC : New Growth Press, 2020. | Audience: Ages 8-11
   | Summary: "WonderFull by best-selling author Marty Machowski captivates
   children, inviting them to engage with the book of Psalms. Oliver and
   his grandfather read through the Psalms together, learning about God's
   love and praying for each other as the seasons change. Even when the
   leaves fall and Oliver's grandfather grows weaker, the Psalms strengthen
   them both to put their trust in God"-- Provided by publisher.
Identifiers: LCCN 2019050149 | ISBN 9781948130745 (hardback)
Subjects: LCSH: Bible. Psalms--Devotional use--Juvenile literature.
Classification: LCC BS1430.54 .M325 2020 | DDC 242/.5--dc23
LC record available at https://lccn.loc.gov/2019050149

Printed in India

29 28 27 26 25 24 23 22   5 6 7 8 9

Dedication

To Bob Kauflin:

Whose music, songwriting, and pastoral care
have blessed the hearts and lives of people across the world.

May the Lord continue to use your gifts to promote the gospel
and introduce young and old to our glorious Christ.

You are the glorious Christ
The greatest of all delights
Your power is unequaled
Your love beyond all heights
No greater sacrifice
Than when You laid down Your life
We join the song of angels
Who praise You day and night
Glorious Christ.
—Bob Kauflin

Contents

Introduction

Wonderfull is designed to help children grow in knowing and loving God through reading the Psalms and learning to use them to guide worship and prayer. It is my hope that in this journey of learning to apply the Psalms to life through prayer you will be amazed at how they connect together. While each psalm carries its own message, its connection with the psalms around it add to the story.

For example, notice how Psalm 23 doesn't stand alone. It follows Psalm 22, which looks ahead to Christ's crucifixion. Thus, we are meant to read "The Lord is my shepherd; I shall not want" in the shadow of the cross. The reason we need not be afraid of the valley of the shadow of death is because our Good Shepherd, Jesus, died for us.

The Psalms, assembled by an editor under the inspiration of the Holy Spirit, comprises 150 songs sung by God's people, Israel. One thousand years passed from the time Moses wrote the earliest psalm until the writing of the most recent. These songs were written by those who trusted God through real-life struggles. Prominent themes are a prayerful dependence on God, hope in God's deliverance, and trust in his salvation.

The psalms are a guide for how to talk to God about hopes, fears, troubles, frustrations, disappointments, and gratitude. As you share this book with your child, you will be starting them on a lifelong journey of learning to talk to God about everything and receiving his comfort, conviction, forgiveness, help, and hope in return. The steadfast love of the Lord never fails!

To help children learn how to use the Psalms as prayers, the book follows the story of a young boy as he learns to pray the Psalms. As you read about Oliver being comforted and helped by the Psalms, encourage your children to pray the Psalms through their own trials and loss.

WonderFull is designed to be read alongside the Bible. Read the designated psalm and then read the corresponding text in *WonderFull*.

WonderFull can be appreciated by a range of ages. The text is written for grade school but the illustrations will help the youngest follow along. You can also encourage your older children to start a journal and keep track of their prayers through the Psalms. The section "A Closer Look" has suggestions for journal entries and other ideas about how to apply the Psalms to their life. Also included at the end of the book for older children is a study guide, "Going Deeper: A WonderFull Study of Twenty-Five Psalms."

Finally, I want to encourage you to read this book slowly. Don't rush through the Psalms. Perhaps read just one at night before bed. Each psalm is a treasure, and the more time you spend on them, the more wonderful you will find them to be. May God bless your family through *WonderFull* as you praise and pray through the Psalms.

Chapter One

Oliver's Story:

Where It All Began

Eleven-year-old Oliver woke to the song of cicadas and the barking of Grandpa's dog, Charlie. Last night, he and his parents made the long journey—leaving behind their home and friends—to help Grandpa on his farm.

Oliver slipped out of bed, got dressed, and tiptoed to the door, so as to not wake his parents. The well-worn wooden floors of the farmhouse squeaked as he opened the bedroom door. Maybe this would be a fresh start—a new school, new friends, and best of all—a place to leave his past behind.

As he peeked out into the hallway, Oliver could see Grandpa's study. The sun shone through the windows and out into the hallway. Like his grandfather, Oliver loved to read. So he walked toward the study, eager to find a good book.

Oliver noticed a table he had knocked over several years ago when chasing Charlie through the house. His parents were not pleased, but Grandpa said, "Life has many troubles, but thankfully this is a small one." Then he smiled at Oliver. Grandpa was always gracious.

As Oliver surveyed Grandpa's library, he couldn't help but notice the sun shining directly on one particular book. Oliver leaned in for a closer look.

On the spine of the book, was the title *WonderFull: Ancient Psalms Ever New*. As he pulled it off the shelf, he noticed a note taped to its cover. It read: A Gift for Oliver.

Oliver's curiosity grew. If it was a gift for him, how long must he wait to read it? Just outside the window was a forest in full bloom, waiting to be explored. It was also the perfect place to read. Oliver tucked the book under his arm, dashed down the hall, threw open the door, and burst outside, leaving the screen door flapping behind him.

Oliver raced down the grassy lawn,
toward the forest. A tangle of honeysuckle
covered the fence, filling the air with its sweet perfume. The birds were flitting
and flying about, and now and again a squirrel or rabbit bounded out of sight.
The leaves in the trees rustled as the wind whistled through their branches.

Oliver spied a fallen log against the foot of an old oak tree—the perfect spot to
read! He sat on the log, and opened the book, eager to begin the story.

Oliver quickly realized the book contained a collection of ancient songs. That
must be why Grandpa chose it for him—because he loved music!

Oliver began by reading Psalm 1. It included an ancient promise and an
eternal blessing—that a man could be like a tree planted by streams of
water, with leaves that would not wither. Oliver loved the idea of trees
being planted by a stream. He looked up at the tree branches and
imagined a world where leaves would never wither or fall.

As Oliver read on, he realized this beautiful promise was only for one group of people—those who turn from their sin. All at once, Oliver's enthusiasm for reading was squelched.

He started to remember the wrong things he had done—particularly, his recent suspension for cheating on a test in school. Reading Psalm 1 reminded him of all of it—not just the cheating, but the stuff beneath it, that led him to do it in the first place. Suddenly, he felt like a character in Psalm 1: the man walking in the counsel of the wicked.

Was there any hope for him?

Cautiously, he continued reading. But his fears were realized when he read the last line of the psalm: *the way of the wicked will perish.*

Grandpa, on a mission for his morning coffee, noticed the screen door ajar. *I'll bet he's off reading,* he thought. Grandpa headed toward his study and immediately noticed the book missing from the shelf. He smiled, slipped on his boots, and left in search of Oliver—knowing just where to find him: in the forest, under the old oak tree.

"I thought I'd find you here!" said Grandpa. "So, tell me—how do you like the book?"

"How did you know where to find me?" asked Oliver.

"You've always loved the forest." For the first time in a while, Oliver felt known and understood. Since Oliver was a young boy, he and Grandpa had been reading books together. But things felt different now. Oliver was sure Grandpa wouldn't approve of his recent behaviors—let alone what was going on in his heart and mind.

"So, do you like the book?" Grandpa asked again.

"Well, I read Psalm 1, and to be honest, it left me feeling pretty hopeless. It made me think about all the things I've done wrong lately."

Grandpa sat beside Oliver and said, "It can feel that way, can't it? Psalm 1 shines a spotlight on our sin, and that is always hard. No one likes to think about what we do wrong. But the good news is that God doesn't treat us as our sins deserve. He is slow to anger and overflowing with love.

Because God is holy, he can't be in the presence of sin. So he sent Jesus, the perfect One—who never walked in the counsel of the wicked, nor followed the path of sinners—to be our Savior. Jesus did what we could never do. He delighted in the law and meditated on it both day and night. He lived a perfect life. And he offers us the greatest exchange of all time—his perfect life and sacrifice for our sin and shame. He trades his perfect record for our sinful one."

Oliver considered his *own* record in comparison to Jesus's perfect one. Was such an exchange even possible?

Grandpa continued, "More than two thousand years ago, Jesus willingly died on the cross, nailed there by sinners like you and me. While on the cross, God the Father poured our punishment upon Jesus. And then Jesus died. But, three days later he rose again from the dead, proving his victory over sin and death— paving the way for our salvation. He is our only hope for forgiveness. He's the only way we can live like the trees planted by the water."

Oliver said, "I have always heard at church that 'Jesus died for your sins,' but I didn't think too much about it." But Oliver was thinking about it now.

Grandpa continued, "Psalm 1 is an invitation to discover the blessings of following God's Word. We all fall short, Oliver. You are not alone in this. But, we can accept God's invitation of grace and forgiveness. We can experience the blessing of walking with him—just like that beautiful picture in Psalm 1."

Oliver wondered:
Is this true? Is there hope for me? Can I really have a fresh start?

Grandpa continued, "You know, *WonderFull* was my favorite book when I was your age. It taught me about God and how to talk to him. It even gave me the words to pray. I read it for the first time out in this same forest, under this same tree."

"Wow," Oliver replied. "This tree must be old!"

Grandpa laughed. "This oak is more than a hundred years old! I might be getting up in age, but I'm not quite there yet. But, I do I have an idea. Would you be interested in reading this book together and reading a new psalm each day?"

"Really?" Oliver asked. "Could we read under this great oak?"

"Sure, I have all the time in the world, and I'd love to spend it reading with you."

"Thanks, Grandpa. I'd love to!"

As Grandpa and Oliver walked back to the farmhouse, Oliver wondered if God might hear his prayers. He only wanted to ask for two things: for a fresh start, and for Grandpa to feel better.

Welcome to the Psalms

In the Psalms, God invites us to know and love his Word. He especially wants us to use it.

Each psalm is a song. The musical melodies are lost, but the words have been preserved in a book. The psalms use poetry to teach important truths about God and ourselves. Often the psalms use word pictures to illustrate something important.

In his psalms, David often shares his feelings with God. Sometimes David is happy, and sometimes sad. There are other times when he's worried or angry. As you go about your day, you can meet with God as you read the Psalms. You can be encouraged that you are not alone, and that just as God helped David, he will help you too.

Think about your day. What are you looking forward to? What can you thank God for? Is there anything you wish weren't happening today? How can you ask for God's help in it?

Book
Nº 1

Psalms 1–41

KING DAVID'S SONGS

Live like a Tree by the Water
READ PSALM 1

Blessed is the man
who walks not in the counsel of the wicked,
nor stands in the way of sinners,
nor sits in the seat of scoffers;
but his delight is in the law of the Lord,
and on his law he meditates day and night.

He is like a tree
planted by streams of water
that yields its fruit in its season,
and its leaf does not wither.
In all that he does, he prospers.
The wicked are not so,
but are like the chaff that the wind drives away.

Therefore the wicked will not stand in the judgment,
nor sinners in the congregation of the righteous;
for the Lord knows the way of the righteous,
but the way of the wicked shall perish.

Here are the words to the very first psalm. What pictures does this psalm use? Imagine being a tree planted by the water. What would be good about that? Now imagine being "chaff" (the useless part of wheat that is so light that the wind blows it away). What would be bad about that?

For a tree, the river bank is the best place to be. Living along a stream gives the tree plenty of water and good soil, even when it doesn't rain for a long time. For a person, living like a tree planted by streams of water means you love God and trust that he cares for you. Even in life's storms God is with you to help you trust him and supply all you need. But those who do not follow God and refuse to trust him will be like the chaff that blows away.

God is calling you to be like a tree planted by streams of water—as you follow Jesus. Jesus obeyed Psalm 1 perfectly. None of us can live perfectly like Jesus, but if we place our trust in Jesus he promises to share his perfect life with us and take away our sin. He will be your rescuer and helper.

When you believe in Jesus and his sacrifice on the cross, his Holy Spirit fills you. He writes God's law upon your heart (Jeremiah 31:33) and helps you to bear good fruit just like the tree.

A Closer Look

Consider keeping a journal for your explorations in the Psalms. With each new entry, write down the psalm number, what you learn about God, and what you learn about yourself. You can start today by asking God to help you become like the righteous person in this psalm—always trusting in Jesus and remembering and practicing God's Word.

A Prophecy about Jesus
READ PSALM 2

I will tell of the decree: The Lord said to me,
"You are my Son; today I have begotten you.
Ask of me, and I will make the nations your heritage,
and the ends of the earth your possession.
　　You shall break them with a rod of iron
and dash them in pieces like a potter's vessel." (vv. 7–9)

Psalm 2 looks far ahead to the future with great joy—a day when God would send his Son to be born on the earth. But, along with this great joy comes great sadness—for many people on the earth will turn against him.

There was one particular man who turned against God's Son, Jesus, shortly after his birth. His name was King Herod (v. 2). He tried to get rid of Jesus the moment he heard of him. Why? Because he was afraid to lose his own power. He wanted to do things his way.

Have you ever, like King Herod, wanted to do things your way, rather than God's way? Have you wondered if you might be a better ruler? Maybe you like to be in charge of everything. Maybe you're afraid of what it might cost, or what you might lose, by following God.

Thankfully God already knows your heart, and he came to rescue sinners. He sent his Son Jesus to die in your place so the curse of sin could be broken—so you might live as a tree planted by streams of water—delighting in following Jesus, rather than trying to go your own way. God invites you to worship and bow before him.

One day, every knee will bow before King Jesus—even those who reject him. But those who trust in the forgiveness of sins through Jesus, are fully and completely forgiven, for all eternity.

Until that day, God calls you to honor him with your life. You can do this every day, wherever you go.

A Closer Look

Look at the last verse of this psalm, "Blessed are all who take refuge in him" (v. 12). A refuge is a safe place. What do you learn about Jesus from this psalm that makes him your best safe place? Ask God to help you remember Jesus is the King of Kings. How could you honor him today?

A Closer Look

Do you ever have trouble falling asleep? What are some things David says about God that you could remember when you are having a hard time going to sleep? If you would like, write them down in your journal to help you remember.

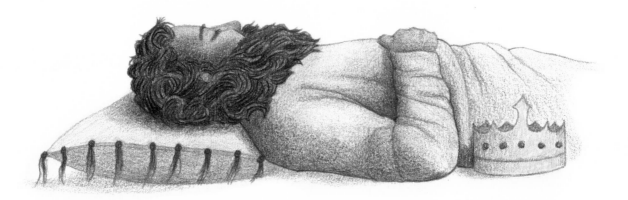

The Psalms Tell Stories
READ PSALM 3

**I lay down and slept;
I woke again, for the Lord sustained me. (v. 5)**

The Psalms are filled with stories and prayers to use in your everyday life. Today's psalm tells the story of a time when King David was sad and crying out to God for help. You can pray this psalm when you are sad and afraid too.

David's son Absalom has turned against him. Each day, he stood at the city gate, turning the people against King David (2 Samuel 15:1–6). He invited an army of men to join his mission (2 Samuel 18:1–5).

Imagine how David must have felt—at war with his own son! But, it was in this moment that David remembered God's promise to him, "I have been with you wherever you went and have cut off all your enemies from before you" (2 Samuel 7:9).

So, that night, while David was having trouble falling asleep, he trusted God's promise and prayed. He then fell asleep in peace—free from all fear. The next day, David's army won the battle against Absalom!

Like David, you face battles too. Perhaps you are tempted to do something wrong, maybe someone is being mean to you, or someone you love might be sick. Whatever your battle, when we are trying to get to sleep our problems can seem even bigger. When that happens, you can, like David, remember God's promises and ask for his help. Where have you seen his help in the past? Consider asking your parents this question as well.

Then, pray along with David: "You, O Lord, are a shield about me, my glory, and the lifter of my head," (Psalm 3:3). God promises to be with you. He is a shield about you and the lifter of your head. He will sustain you.

A Closer Look
Yahweh

O LORD, how many are my foes!
Many are rising against me:
Many are saying of my soul,
"There is no salvation for him in God."

But you,
O
LORD,
are a
shield
about me,
my glory, and the lifter of my head.
I cried aloud to the LORD,
And he answered me from his holy hill.

I lay down and slept;
I woke again, for the LORD sustained me.
I will not be afraid of many thousands of people
who have set themselves against me all around.

Arise, O LORD!
Save me, O my God!
For you strike all my enemies on the cheek;
You break the teeth of the wicked.
Salvation belongs to the LORD:
Your blessing be on your people!

Yahweh—
A Very Special Word

The word LORD (in small capital letters) occurs six times in Psalm 3. See if you can find all of them.

The English word LORD stands for the Hebrew word *Yahweh* (pronounced *yah-way*). Yahweh is the name God told Moses to call him at the burning bush (Exodus 3:15).

God told his people through Moses that no man could see him and live (Exodus 33:20). When God's voice thundered from his holy mountain, the people became afraid. They saw God send plagues and fire to destroy his enemies and correct his people when they strayed from his commandments. The people respected God's holiness and were afraid to even speak the name Yahweh. So, when they read the Bible, they spoke another word for God. They replaced it with the Hebrew word *Adonai*, which means LORD.

This tradition carries forward all the way till today. Instead of writing God's covenant name, Yahweh, many English translations of the Bible substitute the word LORD. The capital letters tell you it is God's covenant name, Yahweh. Now look at Psalm 3 again, this time with the word Yahweh.

God Speaks to You Through the Psalms
READ PSALM 4

But know that the LORD has set apart the godly for himself;
The LORD hears when I call to him. (v. 3)

Do you know you have a teacher who helps you to learn about the Psalms? It is the Holy Spirit. The Holy Spirit is God. God is in three persons: the Father, Son, and Holy Spirit. One of the Holy Spirit's jobs is to help you understand the Bible. Each time you open the Psalms, ask him to speak to you and help you understand what God is saying to you today. He will always help you.

In each psalm the Holy Spirit can help you learn something wonderful about God. And you will also learn about how God loves and helps you. For example, in today's psalm we learn that David trusted God to hear and answer his prayers. When is it easy to believe God hears our prayers? When is it hard?

We also learn that David depends on God to fall asleep. He says, "In peace I will both lie down and sleep; for you alone, O LORD, make me dwell in safety" (v. 8). He trusts God's promises to be true, even in the dark. So, we learn that God is near and trustworthy. Do you believe this? Can you remember a time when you knew God was close? When is it hard to trust God is near?

What did you do today? Where did you go? Before bed share your day with God, just like David did (v. 4). Did you follow and obey God today? If not, tell God you are sorry and ask him to help you live for him tomorrow. He will forgive you for Jesus's sake and help you. Which of God's promises can you remember tonight?

A Closer Look

A good way to learn to how to pray is to rewrite a psalm as your own prayer. You can pick just one verse or a few as your own prayer. Soon, you'll have a journal filled with wonderful truths and prayers! In the very next psalm, we will practice turning the Psalms into our prayers.

The Psalms Help Us Pray
READ PSALM 5

Give ear to my words, O Lord;
consider my groaning.
Give attention to the sound of my cry,

my
King
and God,
my
for to you do I
pray.

O Lord, in the morning you hear my voice;
in the morning I prepare a sacrifice for you and watch.

Did you know you can use the words of the Psalms to help you pray? When you read a psalm, think of ways you could use it in your prayers to God. We have hard days just like the psalm writers did and we need God's help too.

Practice making Psalm 5 your own prayer. Ask the Holy Spirit to help you use David's prayers and make them your own. For example, Psalm 5 might become something like this:

Dear Jesus, you are my King and my God. Please hear my prayer this morning and help me live for you and keep a close watch over all I do.

God, please forgive me for ignoring you today. Forgive me for lying to my parents, and for being mean to my sister. Thank you for forgiveness. Thank you that I can come near to you because of Jesus. Thank you for listening.

This week, I really need your help at school. I'm so tired of the kids being mean. Please speak to them—you know who they are. Be my shield and protector and pave a path for me so I know what to do. Thank you for always being my safe place. Amen.

Now it's your turn! Try reshaping Psalm 5 into your own words and prayer. Share what's really on your heart. Where do you need God's help? Where do you need forgiveness? What are you thankful for? Offer your words to God as a prayer.

A Closer Look

Make a list of all the things that David says that God will do for him in answer to his prayer. Underline one verse from this psalm that you would like to remember today. If you would like, you can put the date next to the verse and your prayer request.

Psalm 11:1

Prayers for Difficult Days
READ PSALMS 6, 7, 9, 10, 11, 12, 13

A lament is a sad prayer or song where the author shares the trouble he or she feels. When sad things happen, the Psalms show us it is okay to tell God how we really feel. God is our loving Father who cares for us and is always ready to comfort us.

King David called out to God in times of trouble, and he even wrote songs about his difficult days for all the people to sing. David prayed to God for protection from his enemies. All through his life there were people who wanted to harm him and also harm Israel. But any of your troubles can be your "enemies." These songs are examples of how we can pray any time we are in any kind of trouble.

Read through Psalms 6, 7, 9, 10, 11, 12, and 13. As you read, remember Jesus is the Lord. Jesus knows how hard the sad days can be—he had sad days of his own. So, the next time something sad or disappointing happens, tell God how you feel. Then, like King David did, ask God for help. You can pray one of these psalms every day. There is no hurry! Take your time.

PSALM 6
A Prayer to God When You Are Sad

"I am weary with my moaning; every night I flood my bed with tears; I drench my couch with my weeping. My eye wastes away because of grief; it grows weak because of all my foes." (vv. 6–7)

Read Psalm 6 from your Bible. Choose a verse or two as a guide and tell God all of the reasons you are sad. Then ask him to help you because of his steadfast love (v. 4). How did praying this way help you?

PSALM 7
A Prayer to God When You Are in Trouble

"O LORD my God, in you do I take refuge; save me from all my pursuers and deliver me." (v. 1)

"My shield is God Most High, who saves the upright in heart." (v. 10 NIV)

Read Psalm 7 from your Bible. What part of David's prayer reminds you of your life and something you are going through? Underline one verse and put the date next to it to remind you you prayed for help. Perhaps next time you read Psalm 7 you will be able to add how God answered your prayer.

PSALM 9
A Prayer for Grace

"Be gracious to me, O LORD! See my affliction from those who hate me." (v. 13)

In this psalm David prays that God will give him grace (help he doesn't deserve). Sometimes the best thing to do on a hard day is to remember what God has already done for you. David does this in Psalm 9. He begins by counting all of God's wonderful deeds. Make a list of ten things God has done for you. Now turn the items on your list into a prayer of thanks and pray it back to God. Then ask for grace for what you are facing today.

PSALM 10
A Prayer for When You Feel Alone

"Why, O LORD, do you stand far away? Why do you hide yourself in times of trouble?" (v. 1)

"To you the helpless commits himself; you have been the helper of the fatherless." (v. 14)

Have you ever felt like God is far away from you? Read through Psalm 10. Even though David feels like God is far away, he prays anyway. How is the end of the psalm different than the beginning (vv. 16–18)? What do you learn about when to pray from this psalm?

PSALM 11
A Prayer for Safety

"In the LORD I take refuge; how can you say to my soul, 'Flee like a bird to your mountain, for behold, the wicked bend the bow; they have fitted their arrow to the string to shoot in the dark at the upright in heart; if the foundations are destroyed, what can the righteous do?'. . . For the LORD is righteous; he loves righteous deeds; the upright shall behold his face." (vv. 1–3, 7)

Notice how David fills his prayer with truths about God. Make a list of three things you want to pray about and three truths about who God is that you can speak back to him in prayer. Then find a quiet place and pray, using both lists.

PSALM 12
A Prayer for When You Are Discouraged

"Save, O Lᴏʀᴅ, for the godly one is gone; for the faithful have vanished from among the children of man. Everyone utters lies to his neighbor; with flattering lips and a double heart they speak." (vv. 1–2)
"Lᴏʀᴅ, keep us safe. Always protect us from such people."
(v. 7 ICB)

"Save" is another word for "rescue." God rescues us from trouble and sin, and he comforts us in our suffering. Where do you need God to save you?

PSALM 13
A Prayer for When You Are Tired of Waiting for God to Help

"How long, O Lᴏʀᴅ? Will you forget me forever? How long will you hide your face from me? How long must I take counsel in my soul and have sorrow in my heart all the day? How long shall my enemy be exalted over me?" (vv. 1–2)
"But I have trusted in your steadfast love; my heart shall rejoice in your salvation." (v. 5)

When we are in trouble, it can seem like God isn't listening to our prayers. David wants God to do something right now! He wants to know "How long?" We can ask those questions too. But in the end we can turn to God, like David did, and say that we trust in "your steadfast love." God can help us wait patiently for the answer to our prayer and to trust God does hear us when we call.

God Is Bigger Than Our Troubles
READ PSALM 8

When I look at your heavens, the work of your fingers, the moon and the stars, which you have set in place, what is man that you are mindful of him, and the son of man that you care for him? (vv. 3–4)

Right in the middle of the psalms that help us pray our troubles, this psalm reminds us how big and powerful God is. He is bigger than any trouble we face. The psalm writer, awed by creation, celebrates the glory and majesty of the Creator. In the New Testament, the writer of Hebrews quotes this psalm and tells us Jesus is the "Son of Man" that David is writing about (Hebrews 2:5–9). Isn't it good to remember Jesus in the midst of our trouble? Jesus lived through difficult days and understands what it feels like to lose friends, be disappointed, made fun of, and even beaten. But Jesus is also the King of the whole world. He rose from the dead and now he sits at the right hand of the Father, praying for us (Hebrews 7:25). This Jesus says to you, "Come to me, all you who are weary and burdened, and I will give you rest" (Matthew 11:28 NIV).

On a clear night, go outside and look at the stars. How small we are compared with the vast reaches of space! Jesus spoke and this world came into being. How powerful must God be to create the planets, stars, and galaxies of outer space! He is more powerful than your troubles and will help you when you ask.

A Closer Look

Write in your journal all of the things you can think of in this world that are bigger than you are. Then next to each one write, "God is bigger than _____." Use this list to remind you God is more powerful and bigger than anything in the universe, and he cares for you.

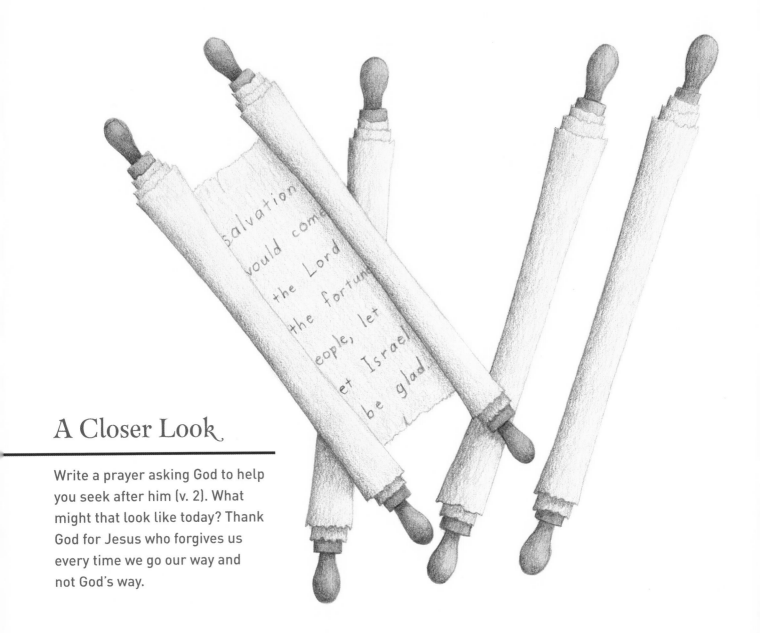

salvation
would com
the Lord
the fortun
eople, let
et Israel
be glad

A Closer Look

Write a prayer asking God to help
you seek after him (v. 2). What
might that look like today? Thank
God for Jesus who forgives us
every time we go our way and
not God's way.

The Bad News Comes First
READ PSALM 14

The LORD looks down from heaven on the children of man,
    to see if there are any who understand,
    who seek after God.
They have all turned aside; together they have
become corrupt;
    there is none who does good,
    not even one. (vv. 2–3)

Have you ever read a book series where each individual book adds more to the greater story? What might happen if you only read one book in the series? What might you miss?

Like books in a series, each psalm makes the most sense when it is read with the psalms before and after it. The person who put the psalms in a book put each one just where he wanted, so they work together. For example, if you read through Psalms 14–16, you might notice each psalm has its own message. Psalm 14 begins with the bad news—that God searched for the righteous and could not find them. Everyone broke his commands and failed to love each other. Psalm 15 goes on to say only perfect people can enter heaven. Let's imagine you stop reading there. What might you think about God? What might you think about yourself?

To read the full story, you have to continue to Psalm 16. God's story doesn't end with imperfect sinners. Instead, Psalm 16 tells us those who trust the Lord will live with him forever in heaven (vv. 10–11). Psalm 16 shares the good news—that God welcomes sinners to salvation. David trusted in this promise of salvation and looked ahead to the coming Savior. Have you trusted in God's gift of salvation through Jesus?

As you continue reading the Psalms, remember to read them as a collection. This way you will see all of the little stories in light of God's greater story of how he saves his people. You will read the bad news that we all do things wrong in light of the Good News that Jesus came to save sinners.

More Bad News
READ PSALM 15

O Lord, who shall sojourn in your tent?
    Who shall dwell on your holy hill? (v. 1)

Have your parents ever told you that you must clean your room before playing outside? Or, have they ever said you need to finish your chores before watching your favorite show? In today's psalm, God shares what you must do before you can go to heaven. And at first glance, it seems way harder than doing a few chores. Actually it seems impossible.

David says that for you to go to heaven, you must be blameless—completely perfect—with no record of mistakes. You must always choose the right way, always tell the truth, love others all the time, keep all your promises, and share with those in need. This means no mean words, no lies, no sin, all day, every day. Can anyone live a perfect life? I know I can't! Thankfully, God already knows we all fall short, and he has provided a better way. He sent Jesus to live a perfect life for us.

Jesus always chose the right way. He spoke the truth, blessed others, kept his promises, and helped those in need. He fulfilled every single requirement of God. He offers to take our sin and give us his perfect record so we can go to heaven. David tells us how he trusted in the Lord in Psalm 16.

When you trust in Jesus and ask him for forgiveness, he does forgive your sins and marks you as blameless. Because Jesus lived a perfect life and offered himself as a sacrifice for sin, you can share in his righteousness and be forgiven. You can be fully and completely accepted by God. Now that's good news!

A Closer Look

Write out a prayer from this psalm.
It might go something like this:
O Lord, help me to do what is right and walk blamelessly before you.
I want to live with you but I've made mistakes. I have sinned by _____ (fill in for yourself).
Please forgive me and help me to believe and trust in your Son, Jesus.

The Secret to the Good News
READ PSALM 16

For you will not abandon my soul to Sheol,
    or let your holy one see corruption. (v. 10)

Verses 9–10 of Psalm 16 contain a secret about something amazing God was going to do. God shared that secret with David many, many years before it happened. Do you know what that secret was?

Here's the secret: Since David died and his body returned to the dust, this psalm could not be talking about him. Psalm 16 points us to Jesus, who died but never saw decay because he rose again on the third day! After Jesus rose from the dead and ascended to heaven, the apostle Peter shares this psalm to prove Jesus is the Messiah (Acts 2:23–28).

In verses 9–10, David tells us about Jesus's life, death, and resurrection many, many years before Jesus is even born! While David didn't know he would be called Jesus, David trusted in God's future plan to send a Savior. For this reason, David has no fear. Instead, he's excited for the future!

Peter, preaching from this psalm, tells us, "Everyone who calls upon the name of the Lord shall be saved" (Acts 2:21). When we believe and put our trust in Jesus, we get to share in David's hope. Now you can be happy as David was: Jesus died and rose again so you might share in his joy and pleasures forever! And that's the best news ever!

A Closer Look

Take some time today to read the resurrection story in one of the four Gospels. As you do so, try to picture the story. Imagine you are hiding along the road, watching everything unfold. You see the Roman soldiers guarding the tomb. You watch as the followers of Jesus race to share the good news of Christ.

Psalm 17:8

Psalm 18:28

Psalm 18:35

Psalm 18:2

The Prayers and Praise of David
READ PSALMS 17–21

David sang and prayed these words to God three thousand years ago! Even though they are very old, they still teach us how to pray to God today. They teach us that God hears our prayers (Psalms 17:6; 18:6). Through reading them we see David trusted God as his Savior (Psalm 18:50) and believed when his eyes closed on the day he died they would open in heaven and he would see God (Psalm 17:15).

Look closely and you can see clues to God's plan to one day save us through his Son Jesus. Psalm 18 speaks of a righteous man who has no sin, but that can't be David. David knows he is a sinner and he needs God to save him and declare him innocent (Psalm 19:12). Even though he didn't know the name Jesus, David trusted in God's plan to save us by redeeming us (Psalm 19:14). The word *redeem* means to "buy back." Jesus did "buy back" our lives from death. He paid the ultimate price by giving up his life. He took the punishment we deserved so we could be forgiven and set free. While David didn't know God's Redeemer would be called Jesus, he trusted in God's plan of salvation to save him from his sins (Psalm 20:6–7). Because of this, David believed he would live forever with God in heaven (Psalm 21:4–6).

As you read these psalms, you will notice David uses word pictures to help us understand what God is like and all the ways he loves and protects us. Circle all the word pictures in your Bible that help you understand God and his love.

PSALM 17
God Answers Our Prayers

"I call upon you, for you will answer me, O God; incline your ear to me; hear my words." Psalm 17:6
"Keep me as the apple of your eye; hide me in the shadow of your wings." Psalm 17:8

David tells God what he believes about him. Tell God what you believe about him using David's words. Everything David says about God is true today and forever!

PSALM 18
God Hears Our Cry for Help

"The LORD is my rock and my fortress and my deliverer, my God, my rock, in whom I take refuge." Psalm 18:2

"In my distress I called upon the LORD; to my God I cried for help. From his temple he heard my voice, and my cry to him reached his ears." Psalm 18:6

When something bad happens to us, we can get angry, blame God, and turn away from him, or we can run to him for help. What did David do? How can David's prayer help you to pray when you are sad and upset?

PSALM 19
Let God's Word Guide Your Prayers

"Let the words of my mouth and the meditation of my heart be acceptable in your sight, O LORD, my rock and my redeemer." Psalm 19:14

Verse 14 is a wonderful prayer to pray every day for the rest of your life. Because the Lord is your rock and your redeemer you can be sure he will help you say and think those things that please him. Memorize this verse and make it your morning prayer.

PSALM 20
Trust in the Lord

"Now I know that the LORD saves his anointed; he will answer him from his holy heaven with the saving might of his right hand. Some trust in chariots and some in horses, but we trust in the name of the LORD our God." Psalm 20:6–7

Did you know you can use the Psalms to pray for your friends and family? Make a list of those you know who need prayer. Use the words of Psalm 20 to help you pray for that person. Insert their name each time you see the word "you" or "your."

PSALM 21
Jesus Is Our Eternal King

"He asked life of you; you gave it to him, length of days forever and ever. His glory is great through your salvation; splendor and majesty you bestow on him. For you make him most blessed forever; you make him glad with the joy of your presence." Psalm 21:4–6

Psalm 21 is a prayer of thanksgiving. Even though David experienced lots of hard times, he never forgot the blessings God gave him. What are some of the blessings God has given you? Use Psalm 21 as a guide and pray them back to God thanking him for each one.

A Closer Look

You can turn to Jesus with your own struggles.
Because he sufferered, you can be sure he understands how you feel.
Thank him for understanding. Thank him for leaving heaven to suffer in your place.
Ask him to help you trust that no matter what trials you face, he will never leave you;
he will *always* be with you (Hebrews 13:5).

A Look Ahead to the Cross
READ PSALM 22:1–11

My God, my God, why have you forsaken me? (v. 1)

In today's psalm, David is on the run, with his enemy, King Saul, trailing close behind. Saul wants to kill him. As David runs and hides, he cries out to God day and night. But, God is not answering. Where is he? Why isn't he helping?

Have you ever asked questions like these? Have you cried out to God and wondered if he is there—and if he is listening? Take heart, David did too. And David was not the only one.

Take a moment to reread Psalm 22:1. Does it sound familiar? Have you read these words anywhere else in Scripture? One thousand years later a crowd is mocking Jesus. Soldiers press a crown of thorns upon his head and beat his body. They flog him with whips and nail him to a wooden cross. They lift the cross high, leaving him to die. As darkness covers the land, Jesus cries these same words from verse 1, "My God, my God why have you forsaken me?" (Matthew 27:46).

Although David wrote Psalm 22 about the trials of his own life, the Holy Spirit helped him write words that also point ahead to the suffering of Christ. Both Jesus and David were despised and mocked. They both felt alone. And they both turned to God the Father for help.

. . . they have pierced

my
hands
and
feet.

Psalm 22:16

And the soldiers twisted together a crown of thorns and put it on his head and arrayed him in a purple robe. They came up to him, saying, "Hail, King of the Jews!" and struck him with their hands.
John 19:2–3

They put a staff in his right hand. Then they knelt in front of him and mocked him.
Matthew 27:29 (NIV)

Psalm 22 is a picture of the future. Long before the life and death of Jesus, David wrote these words, and each of them came true in John 19. It was all part of God's plan (Acts 2:23).

The Gospels tell the sad story of Jesus's crucifixion, but that is not the end. They also give us the hope of salvation. In Matthew 27, Jesus is surrounded by those who want to hurt him. They mock and ridicule him. In John 19, Jesus is pierced in his hands and feet. His clothes are divided and sold. His friends betray him.

Jesus took on your sin and shame so you might receive the gift of salvation. He did this because he loves you and wants to give you forgiveness and eternal life. Have you trusted in Christ to forgive your sins? How can you thank him today for the gift of salvation?

A Closer Look

Bookmark Psalm 22 in your Bible and then turn to turn to John 19 and Matthew 27. Flip back and forth and search for similarities. Look for matching words, phrases, and sentences. What do you notice? Write down the similarities and differences in your journal.

Your Name Is Hidden in This Psalm

READ PSALM 22:22–31

For he has not despised or abhorred
    the affliction of the afflicted,
and he has not hidden his face from him,
    but has heard, when he cried to him. (v. 24)

Psalm 22 has so many wonderful truths in it that we are going to keep thinking about it! Did you know that it wasn't only written for the people of Israel? It was also written for you. When David says God is calling the *coming generation*—he is speaking into the future and including you. Even more amazing, he welcomes the entire world! God's plan has always been to invite every nation and tribe to be saved. Heaven will be filled with people from every corner of the world (Psalm 22:27; Revelation 7:9–10).

Even though you and I were not born when David wrote this psalm, we are a part of God's plan. If you look closely you will see your name hidden in the words of Psalm 22 when you read, "it shall be told of the Lord to the coming generation; they shall come and proclaim his righteousness *to a people yet unborn*, that he has done it" (vv. 30–31 emphasis added). Do you see how you are a part of God's plan in the words David shared?

God wrote the names of everyone he planned to save in a special book called "the book of life" (Revelation 13:8). David foretold that Jesus died for "those yet unborn." The book of life is filled with their names—the names of everyone who God planned to rescue from their sin. The Bible tells us that we can be sure our name is written there if we turn away from our sin and believe in Jesus.

As you think about *The Book of Life* and imagine the many names listed, who do you want to see included? Is there a friend or family member who hasn't yet trusted in Christ? How can you share God's message of hope with them?

A Closer Look

How can you share the gospel message with those who don't know Jesus around the world? Ask your parents or pastor for ideas if you need help. As a follower of Jesus, God invites you to share the good news of Jesus with everyone everywhere!

The Book of Life

Charlie
Maria
Aakash
Chao
Tyler
Chen
Raul
Biming

Dwayne
Theo
Ahmed
Aurora
Finn
Abrahim
Minerva
Norah
Rachel
Sabina

The Book of Life

Michael
Lachlan
Uday
[Your Name here]

Jane
Lucinda
Aiko
Cho

Jesus Is Our Shepherd
READ PSALM 23

The LORD is my shepherd; I shall not want.
  He makes me lie down in green pastures.
He leads me beside still waters.
  He restores my soul.
He leads me in paths of righteousness
  for his name's sake.
Even though I walk through the valley of the shadow of death,
  I will fear no evil,
for **you are with me;**
  your rod and your staff,
  they comfort me.

You prepare a table before me
  in the presence of my enemies;
you anoint my head with oil;
  my cup overflows.
Surely goodness and mercy shall follow me
  all the days of my life,
and I shall dwell in the house of the LORD
  forever.

Imagine you are traveling with your family to a new city. Although you've never visited this city, your parents have, and you know you can trust them. So you follow them onto the train and the platform, through long corridors and stairwells, and across crowded streets. They watch over you closely (and you keep checking to make sure they are nearby) until you get back home. You could say they are shepherding you around the city, just as a shepherd cares for his sheep. Shepherds watch over, lead, and protect those in their flock. Shepherds are always with their sheep.

In Psalm 23 David calls the Lord his shepherd (v. 1). When Jesus came to earth he explained to the people that he was the shepherd David was talking about (John 10:14). He leads, comforts, and protects his sheep (that's you!) through every day, week, month, and year. As you follow your Good Shepherd, you have nothing to fear. Jesus says, "Peace I leave with you; my peace I give to you. Not as the world gives do I give to you. Let not your hearts be troubled, neither let them be afraid" (John 14:27). Because he loves you, he walks with you and watches over you.

Most important of all, our Good Shepherd, Jesus, laid down his life for us (John 10:11). A Good Shepherd is willing to give up his life to save his sheep from their enemies like lions and wolves. Jesus died on the cross to save us from sin and death. That's what Psalm 22 is all about. We can rest in the Shepherd's care (Psalm 23) because by his death on the cross (Psalm 22) Jesus defeated our greatest enemies—sin and death—to bring us peace.

David says to God, "You are with me" (v. 4). This is the promise we all need to remember every day. How do you need Jesus to be with you today? Ask Jesus to watch over you today and to remind you that because he is close you don't have to fear any evil.

A Closer Look

Rewrite Psalm 23 as a prayer to Jesus. Thank Jesus for all the ways he has taken care of you and ask him to watch over you today. Tell him about anything you are worried or fearful about.

More Prayers and Praise of David
READ PSALMS 24–31

We can learn a lot about God from reading King David's psalms. In these psalms we find out that God is our Mighty King of Glory (Psalm 24:10), our rock and strong fortress (Psalm 31), and the one who saves us from trouble (Psalm 27:1). God is holy (Psalm 29:2), the eternal King (Psalm 29:10), and he is faithful (Psalm 26:3).

We also learn about our relationship with God. We can trust him (Psalm 28:7), take refuge in him in times of trouble (Psalm 31:2), call out to him to forgive our sins (Psalm 25:18), and ask him to heal us (Psalm 30:2). Just like David, we can pray these same prayers. We can pray, "O Lord, teach me your paths" from Psalm 25 or "In you, O Lord, I take refuge" from Psalm 31. Take a moment to think about what words from these psalms you would like to pray today. In the Psalms God tells us about himself and gives us words we can pray back to him. You can pray out loud, silently, or even write your prayers down.

Psalm 24
Shout and Sing God's Praises

"Who is he, this King of glory? The LORD Almighty— he is the King of glory." Psalm 24:10 (NIV)

The Psalms are filled with praises to God. Try reading Psalm 24:8–10 out loud five times in a row. Find a quiet place where you are alone, then start with a whisper and end by shouting praises back to God. Doesn't it feel good to shout God's praises?

Psalm 25
Ask God to Lead You

"Lead me in your truth and teach me, for you are the God of my salvation; for you I wait all the day long." Psalm 25:5

Read through Psalm 25 and then use it as your prayer to God. Add in details about your struggles, also add in confession of your own sin as you pray through each line.

Psalm 26
Pray for God's Help

"Prove me, O LORD, and try me; test my heart and my mind. For your steadfast love is before my eyes, and I walk in your faithfulness." Psalm 26:2–3

God chose David to be king of Israel because David loved him. God said David was "a man after my own heart" (Acts 13:22). What are some things David says in this psalm that tell you about how much he loves God? What are some things you do and say just because you love God?

Psalm 27
Do Not Be Afraid

"The LORD is my light and my salvation; whom shall I fear? The LORD is the stronghold of my life; of whom shall I be afraid?"
Psalm 27:1

There is power in declaring what we believe about God. What does David say he believes about God in this psalm? What David believes about God gives him a different perspective on his fears. Read David's positive faith declaration in Psalm 27, then write out one of your own. Think of three things about God you know are true. Now add at the end of each "of whom shall I be afraid?"

Psalm 28
Trust God and Give Thanks

"The LORD is my strength and my shield; my heart trusts in him, and he helps me. My heart leaps for joy, and with my song I praise him."
Psalm 28:7 (NIV)

Why does David's heart "leap for joy" in this psalm? What three verses from Psalm 28 can you make into your own prayer to God? Once you find them, use them to guide you in forming a prayer to God.

Psalm 29
Give God Glory

"Ascribe to the LORD the glory due his name; worship the LORD in the splendor of holiness."
Psalm 29:2

To ascribe God glory means to give or assign glory to God—to praise him for his works. Make a list of all the things God has done for you; then write your own psalm giving praise to God for who he is and what he has done.

Psalm 30
Praise the Lord

"Sing praises to the LORD, O you his saints, and give thanks to his holy name. For his anger is but for a moment, and his favor is for a lifetime."
Psalm 30:4–5

Many of the Psalms call us to sing praises to God. Singing is one of the best ways to spend time with God. Pick your favorite worship song and sing it in the morning when you first get up as a way to follow the call of Psalm 30.

Psalm 31
Take Refuge in God

"In you, O LORD, do I take refuge; let me never be put to shame; in your righteousness deliver me! Incline your ear to me; rescue me speedily! Be a rock of refuge for me, a strong fortress to save me!"
Psalm 31:1–2

The Psalms give us many examples of prayers to help us see ways to call out to God for help. Read Psalm 31 and ask God to help you using some of the words you find there.

How to Ask God for Forgiveness (Part 1)
READ PSALM 32

I acknowledged my sin to you,
  and I did not cover my iniquity;
I said, "I will confess my transgressions to the Lord,"
  and you forgave the iniquity of my sin. (v. 5)

Do you ever find it hard to tell God you have done something wrong? It sure seems easier to hide our sins and pretend we haven't done anything bad. David went through this as well. This psalm is his story of a time when he first tried to ignore his sins, but he finally confessed his sins to God.

David thought if he hid his sin, it would just disappear. But did it? No. Instead, it was the only thing he could think about! Sin is like that. Instead of it disappearing, it keeps reminding you of what you've done.

Maybe you, like David, have done something wrong. You know it's wrong, but you don't want to get in trouble. The sin might feel embarrassing, or you might be afraid of disappointing God and your parents. You might be afraid of getting in trouble. But this psalm shows us the best way of dealing with our sins.

David confessed his sin to God—he brought it into the light—and God immediately forgave him! He was free of all judgment and guilt. He was free of that constant feeling of shame. David was relieved and reminded of the truth—in God there is forgiveness for sins!

We know even more than David about the forgiveness of sins. David looked forward to a Messiah who would save his people, but we can look back and remember our Savior has come. Jesus died for all of our sins. And when he rose again, that was God saying, "Yes! I accept your death as payment for all who believe in you." So when you sin, you don't need to cover it up. You can remember Jesus forgives you and quickly admit it to God and anyone you might have hurt.

A Closer Look

Write a prayer of confession in your journal using
Psalm 32 as a guide. Read 1 John 1:7–9 and add
that into your prayer as well.

Learning about God from David
READ PSALMS 33–41

King David often included declarations (announcements) in the Psalms to tell everyone the things he knew about God. When David wrote these songs, the Holy Spirit helped him know what to say. That is why we can trust everything David wrote about God is true. And since God is the same today as he was in David's day, we can trust and hold onto these same promises. Read through Psalms 33–41 and see what you can learn about God. How do these passages help you grow in your love and trust of the Lord?

PSALM 33
Fear the Lord

"Let all the earth fear the LORD; let all the inhabitants of the world stand in awe of him! For he spoke, and it came to be; he commanded, and it stood firm." Psalm 33:8–9

Remembering all the amazing things God has done is a great way to get excited about praising God. What has God done for you? Make a list of at least three things and then use them to praise God. Use David's praise as a guide to create your own.

PSALM 34
Share God's Deliverance

"I sought the LORD, and he answered me and delivered me from all my fears. Those who look to him are radiant, and their faces shall never be ashamed. This poor man cried, and the LORD heard him and saved him out of all his troubles." Psalm 34:4–6

The Spirit of God often points out a verse to us as we read the Bible. Read through this psalm and ask God to tell you which verse of the psalm he is speaking to you today. Use that verse to guide your prayers, thoughts, and plans for today.

PSALM 35
Declare God's Praises

"Let those who delight in my righteousness shout for joy and be glad and say evermore, 'Great is the Lord, who delights in the welfare of his servant!'" Psalm 35:27

David often asked God to fight his battles and defend him against his enemies. We all have battles—sometimes with enemies, and sometimes with sad things that have happened. Ask God to fight for you. Then remember to thank him when he delivers you.

PSALM 36
Speak of God's Love

"How precious is your steadfast love, O God! The children of mankind take refuge in the shadow of your wings. They feast on the abundance of your house, and you give them drink from the river of your delights." Psalm 36:7–8

The first six verses of Psalm 36 describe the wicked while verses 7–10 describe those who live for God. Think about all the wonderful things God gives to those who trust him. Can you also say "how precious is your steadfast love"? Ask God to help you remember how wonderful it is to know his love and to keep you from being like the wicked who don't fear (worship and love) God.

PSALM 37
Encouragement to Trust God

"Delight yourself in the Lord, and he will give you the desires of your heart." Psalm 37:4

Psalm 37 is filled with great verses to memorize. Choose one of the following three parts to memorize and use in your prayers this week. Psalm 37:4–6, or 7–8, or 18–19, or 23–24.

PSALM 38
Call to God in Trouble

"Do not forsake me, O Lord! O my God, be not far from me! Make haste to help me, O Lord, my salvation!" Psalm 38:21–22

God disciplines those he loves. That means sometimes he allows us to experience consequences when we sin. Read David's lament in this psalm. What is David's hope even though he knows he is a sinner? And in the end what does David choose to follow (v. 20)?

PSALM 39
Confess Your Sin to the Lord

"And now, O Lord, for what do I wait? My hope is in you. Deliver me from all my transgressions. Do not make me the scorn of the fool!" Psalm 39:7–8

God doesn't expect us to get rid of our sin on our own. After his confession David asks God to help him get rid of his sin in verse 8. How does Jesus get rid of sin for you? Look at Romans 5:6–9. Follow David's example. Confess your sins to God and then ask him to forgive you for Jesus's sake.

PSALM 40
Share Your Story

"I waited patiently for the Lord; he inclined to me and heard my cry. He drew me up from the pit of destruction, out of the miry bog, and set my feet upon a rock, making my steps secure. He put a new song in my mouth, a song of praise to our God. Many will see and fear, and put their trust in the Lord." Psalm 40:1–3

David begins Psalm 40 saying he "waited patiently for the Lord." God doesn't answer our prayers in our time; he answers our prayers in his time. What are you waiting for? How does this psalm help you to wait?

PSALM 41
Declare God's Promises

"Blessed is the one who considers the poor! In the day of trouble the Lord delivers him; the Lord protects him and keeps him alive; he is called blessed in the land; you do not give him up to the will of his enemies. The Lord sustains him on his sickbed; in his illness you restore him to full health." Psalm 41:1–3

David's prayers are conversations with God. When he was sick, he prayed for healing. When he was oppressed by his enemies, he prayed for deliverance. God is ready to hear your prayer. What is going on in your life that you could talk to God about today in your prayers?

I sought the LORD,
and he answered me

and

delivered

me from

all
my fears.

Psalm 34:4

Chapter Two

Oliver's Story:

Oliver Has a Change of Heart

One month later, Grandpa closed the book and said, "Well, that's the end of Book One. We've already read through forty-one psalms!"

"I think I'm beginning to understand God's love and how to talk to him in prayer. Also, I'm learning that if I delight in the Lord, he will give me the desires of my heart."

"Psalm 37:4," Grandpa replied.

Oliver then noticed Grandpa's face. He looked older today, or at least more tired. "Grandpa, I'm praying God will heal your body. That's the desire of my heart. I have been praying Psalm 41:3 for you every day this past week."

Oliver gently hugged his grandfather and prayed the verse again, "The LORD sustains him on his sickbed; in his illness you restore him to full health."

Grandpa could see the Psalms at work in Oliver's heart. The two of them sat silently on the log for several minutes. The branches of the great oak swayed above them. Then Grandpa said, "Oliver, my prayers have changed since I was first diagnosed with cancer. At first, I prayed Psalm 6, because I was afraid and needed the peace of Christ. But now I pray through Psalm 16 because I am trusting in the Lord's presence. I know he will sustain me, whatever comes. Let me tell you a story."

"Do you remember the story of Lazarus from the Bible?" Grandpa asked.

"He sounds familiar."

"Well, Lazarus and his sisters, Mary and Martha, were good friends of Jesus. So, when Lazarus became ill, his sisters called for Jesus to come. They desperately wanted his help. They wanted him to heal Lazarus. But instead Jesus took several days to arrive, and by that time, Lazarus had already died.

"In John 11:21–26, Martha saw Jesus walking up the road she said, 'Lord, if you had been here, my brother would not have died.' Jesus comforted Martha, saying that Lazarus would rise again. Then Jesus told her, 'I am the resurrection and the life. Whoever believes in me, though he die, yet shall he live, and everyone who lives and believes in me shall never die.' And then Jesus raised Lazarus from the dead."

Oliver asked, "Why didn't Jesus arrive sooner? He could have healed Lazarus."

"Well, Oliver, physical healing on earth is temporary. It doesn't last forever. But, the forgiveness of sins through Christ is eternal. If God healed my cancer, it would only be for a short time. When Jesus calls me home to heaven, it will be forever. Because Jesus conquered sin and death and rose from the dead, so will I. Jesus is the author of resurrection life—and that's far greater than physical healing."

Oliver knew one thing for sure: "I want to be there with you, Grandpa. I want to live forever with God. I believe what I've read in the Psalms. I believe in his promises."

Grandpa could sense the Spirit at work in Oliver's heart. He asked, "Are you ready to turn from your sins and trust Jesus?"

"Yes, I am."

As they sat upon the log, under the great oak tree, Grandpa led Oliver in a simple prayer of confession. For the first time, Oliver confessed his sins outloud: his cheating, his hiding, and his struggle with temptation. As he did, a weight seemed to lift right off his shoulders. He was not only given a fresh start but an entirely new beginning: he was fully and completely forgiven!

Grandpa and Oliver hugged each other and smiled.
Grandpa said, "It is the greatest joy to know one day
you will be with me in heaven!"

Oliver smiled. Fresh tears of joy trickled from
his eyes. Grandpa rejoiced—knowing that God
had heard and answered his prayers. After several
minutes, Grandpa said, "We can start Book Two
tomorrow, if you'd like!"

"Absolutely!" Oliver answered.

Book
№̱ 2

Psalms 42–72

LET THE NATIONS PRAISE

Thirsty for God
READ PSALM 42

As a deer pants for flowing streams,
so pants my soul for you, O God. (v. 1)

Imagine you are hiking with your family on a hot summer day. After hiking for most of the morning, you are very thirsty. As you round a hill, you see a stream of cool, clean water bubbling out of a spring and flowing down over the rocks. You long for a nice, cool drink. You crave it so much, that you can't think of anything else.

The author of Psalm 42 longs for something, too, but it's not water. Just like a deer is thirsty for water on a hot day, he tells us that he is thirsty for God. In fact, nothing will satisfy him except spending time in God's presence in the house of God—the temple in Jerusalem. The problem is that he is living in a far-off land, far away from God.

Have you ever longed for time with God? Do you have a special spot where you can meet with him in prayer, or to read his Word? It could be anywhere—just you and him. He wants you to long for time with him. He wants you to crave it above all the other things in life—above friends, toys, and even summer vacation.

Take a few minutes now to be still before God. Turn off all devices and distractions and just be quiet. In the quietness, ask God to help your heart long for him.

This week, when you grow thirsty and want something to drink, think about God and, how much you need him, just like you need water. Spend time talking with him each day before the day begins. Ask him for help and strength to face the day.

A Closer Look

Psalms use images or word pictures from the world around us to help us understand God and ourselves. Write down some of the word pictures in this psalm. How do they help you understand yourself? How do they help you understand God?

Hope in God
READ PSALM 43

Why are you cast down, O my soul,
    and why are you in turmoil within me?
Hope in God; for I shall again praise him,
    my salvation and my God. (v. 5)

Remember how the Psalms are like books in a series, each connected to the others? Today's psalm is like that. It continues with the idea of thirsting for God, just like the psalm before it. It even repeats some of the very same words.

The author of this psalm thirsts for God because he feels alone in his faith. The people around him do not love God. Instead, they make fun of him for his faith. It is like he's stranded on an island, far away from home, surrounded by crashing waves. Where can he turn for help? What can he do?

Have you ever felt alone in your faith? Maybe you are the only believer in your family, or in your class at school, or on your sports team. Or maybe you've been made fun of or misunderstood for following Jesus. Not only does the author of Psalm 43 understand, but so does Jesus. He was regularly misunderstood and rejected too.

How did Jesus and the author of today's psalm respond to rejection? They chose to turn to God in prayer and they longed to spend time talking to him. They trusted God's Word. They set their hope on God, not on the words or opinions of other people.

You might face days when people treat you poorly because of your faith in God. You might be tempted to trust their words rather than God's. You might feel confused and sad. When this happens, turn to God and remember what's true. Think about what he says in this psalm in your mind like it's your favorite song. Hope in God. He is your salvation, and you will again praise him.

A Closer Look

Compare Psalms 42 and 43 and
write down all the repeated words you
can find.

Your throne, O God
is
forever
and ever.

The scepter of your kingdom
is a scepter of uprightness...

Psalm 45:6

Grateful Praises
READ PSALMS 44–49

God has a special plan for each one of us. The Bible tells us God planned good works for us to walk in even before we were born (Ephesians 2:10). Long ago, when God spared the sons of Korah, he knew one day they would write and sing beautiful songs. The psalms of the sons of Korah are filled with grateful praises. God also blessed these men with a prophetic gift so some of their songs, like Psalm 45:6–7, point down through time to Jesus. We can use the words the Holy Spirit inspired in those who wrote them to guide our prayers. The Psalms are God's words we can speak back to him. In the Psalms God speaks to us and then we can speak his words back to him as our prayers. Whenever you are not sure what to pray, try starting with one of the praises of the sons of Korah.

PSALM 44
God Is All Powerful

"O God, we have heard with our ears, our fathers have told us, what deeds you performed in their days, in the days of old: you with your own hand drove out the nations, but them you planted; you afflicted the peoples, but them you set free; for not by their own sword did they win the land, nor did their own arm save them, but your right hand and your arm, and the light of your face, for you delighted in them." (vv. 1–3)

A great way to build our faith in God is to remember what he has done for us and put those thoughts together to form a prayer. Make a list of all God has done for you and use that list to praise him and so by grow your faith for his work in your future.

PSALM 45
God Is Righteous

"Your throne, O God, is forever and ever. The scepter of your kingdom is a scepter of uprightness; you have loved righteousness and hated wickedness. Therefore God, your God, has anointed you with the oil of gladness beyond your companions." (vv. 6–7 and quoted in Hebrews 1:8–9 to describe Jesus)

Think about eternity; forever and ever with no end and allow it to fill your prayers with hope and joy. In spite of our trials now, we know those who give their lives to Jesus will live with him forever in a new earth free from trouble.

PSALM 46
God Is Our Refuge

"God is our refuge and strength, a very present help in trouble. Therefore we will not fear though the earth gives way, though the mountains be moved into the heart of the sea, though its waters roar and foam, though the mountains tremble at its swelling." (vv. 1–3)

How can the truth found in the first two verses of this psalm encourage you when you are going through a tough time?

PSALM 47
God Rules over the Earth

"Sing praises to God, sing praises! Sing praises to our King, sing praises! For God is the King of all the earth; sing praises with a psalm!" (vv. 6–7)

It is important to remember the Psalms are songs. When we read a psalm that encourages us to sing, we should sing! Do you have a favorite worship song you love to sing to God? If so, sing it out in your quiet time. If not, ask others what their favorite one is.

PSALM 48
God Is Eternal

"Walk about Zion, go around her, number her towers, consider well her ramparts, go through her citadels, that you may tell the next generation that this is God, our God forever and ever. He will guide us forever." (vv. 12–14)

The writer of Psalm 48 is amazed at the magnificence of the city of Jerusalem. He wants everyone to know about God—even the youngest children and those not yet born. If you had a son or daughter, what would you tell them God has done for you? Turn your answer into a prayer of thanks to God.

PSALM 49
Only God Can Pay Our Ransom

"Truly no man can ransom another, or give to God the price of his life, for the ransom of their life is costly and can never suffice, that he should live on forever and never see the pit." (vv. 7–9)

We will all one day stand before God and give account for our lives. Jesus paid our debt of sin with his life so all who trust in Jesus can be ransomed from certain death. Are you trusting in Jesus and what he has done on the cross to ransom you (pay your debt) so you might live in heaven with him?

God is
our
refuge
and
strength,

a very present help in trouble.

Psalm 46

Your New Song

READ PSALM 50

"Offer to God a sacrifice of thanksgiving,
    and perform your vows to the Most High,
and call upon me in the day of trouble;
    I will deliver you, and you shall glorify me." (vv. 14–15)

Have you ever watched a musical, where the story is set to music? Rather than speak out all their lines, the characters *sing* them! Psalm 50 is like that. When God gave a message to men like David and Asaph, they often chose to write songs to share God's Word with the people. What a unique way to share and hear God's message!

Asaph wrote the words and music of today's psalm, and in it, he shared something very important. He said God isn't impressed by good works or outward behavior. Back then, God didn't want Israel to sacrifice to him because it was the right thing to do. God wanted them to sacrifice out of their love for him. You see, God cares more about our hearts—what's happening inside of us.

So what about us? Do we pray, learn Bible verses, or go to church just because it is the right thing to do, or do we do these things because we love God and want to worship him? Like Israel, God wants us to love him with all of our hearts. God desires that we pray and worship him out of love for what he has done for us. And the most amazing thing God has done was sending his only Son Jesus to die in our place so we could be forgiven.

Psalm 50 reminds us God loves us, and because he loves us he will help us in our day of trouble. He wants us to *love* him back with all of our heart.

A Closer Look

Write a prayer using Psalm 50 as your guide.
Here is a suggestion: "Help me to live a life of *love*,
not one seeking approval. Amen."

A Closer Look

Here are some other Bible verses to look up that will remind you that because of Jesus, God will forgive your sins: Matthew 26:28; Luke 24:46–47; Acts 2:38; Colossians 1:13–15; 1 John 1:9. Which one is your favorite verse?

How to Ask God for Forgiveness (Part 2)
READ PSALM 51

Have mercy on me, O God,
    according to your steadfast love;
according to your abundant mercy
    blot out my transgressions. (v. 1)

Have you ever been caught doing something you're not supposed to? How did you respond? Were you embarrassed or angry? Did you make excuses? In this psalm, David is caught in his sin, and he must decide what to do.

One day, David hears a knock on his door. It's the prophet Nathan who has come to confront David. Nathan knows all about David's secret sins. He knows David wanted to marry a woman who was already married, and he arranged for her husband to be killed. Then, David married her.

David saw what he did was wrong and confessed, "I have sinned against the LORD," (2 Samuel 12:13) he told Nathan.

Psalm 51 is David's confession put to music. When you are caught in a sin, you can use David's prayer to help you know how to ask God for forgiveness.

David didn't make excuses, he knew he sinned against God—we see that in verses 3–4. David also knew God could take away his sin (vv. 1, 2, 7, and 10). David humbled himself by sharing his confession with all the people of Israel through this song. He hoped we could learn from his mistake (v. 13). Whenever we sin, we can follow David's prayer and admit our wrong and ask God to forgive us. That will be every day!

We know even more about the forgiveness of sins today than David did. We know for sure that God will forgive us because Jesus paid for our sins when he died on the cross. When you tell God you are sorry for your sins (repent) and trust in Jesus, you can be sure you are forgiven by God. He won't hold your sin against you. Do you have any sins to confess to God today? Where do you need forgiveness? God welcomes you to walk in the light, just like David.

What to Do about Your Enemies
READ PSALM 52

Why do you boast of evil, O mighty man?
  The steadfast love of God endures all the day. (v. 1)

Has anyone ever turned *against* you? Maybe kids are being mean at the playground, at school, or in your neighborhood. When this happens, are you tempted to fight back, or be mean in return? King Saul turned against David and wanted to destroy him. But David didn't fight back. He trusted God to defend him against his enemies. That is what Psalm 52 is about.

There is a story behind Psalm 52, Saul and his followers named Doeg the Edomite turn against David and kill his friends, the priests. Even so, David still trusts God. He knows Saul is God's anointed king. He also knows only God can win the battle against evil. David knows God will judge Doeg for his evil ways. Psalm 52 is a song of judgment against Doeg for the sinful things he did.

God gave us Psalm 52 to teach us that we can trust God to punish evil. It is also a warning to us to be sure to treat others with kindness. We must remember God is holy and will judge and punish sin. But, if we do sin, we should also remember Jesus died on the cross for the sins of everyone who will place their trust in him. We can be forgiven if we turn away from our sin and believe Jesus died in our place.

Today, talk with your parents about a difficult situation or person you are facing. Has someone bullied or turned against you? Or, have you been unkind to anyone? Talk with your parents about how to respond in love and also what it might look like to trust God like David did.

1 Samuel 21:9

A Closer Look

Jesus tells us to love our enemies (Luke 6:27). Isn't that strange? But that's exactly what Jesus did when he gave his life for his people. The Bible tells us Jesus didn't die for his friends. He died so his enemies could become his friends (Romans 5:8–10). Now that's good news! Ask God to help you love your enemies like Jesus did.

A Twin Psalm for the Nations
READ PSALM 53

Oh, that salvation for Israel would come out of Zion! (v. 6)

Did you ever meet a set of identical twins? It can be very hard to tell them apart because they look just like each other. Psalm 53 has a twin psalm: Psalm 14. The two psalms are nearly the same. Compare the beginning of verse 2 from both psalms. Can you find the difference?

**"The Lord looks down from heaven on the children of man."
Psalm 14:2**

**"God looks down from heaven on the children of man."
Psalm 53:2**

Psalm 53 changes the words "The Lord" to "God." There is an interesting reason. "The Lord" in small capital letters in Psalm 14 stands for *Yahweh*, the covenant name for the God of Israel. The word "God" in Psalm 53 is the Hebrew word *Elohim*. God's people used that word to describe God over all the nations of the earth. Psalm 14 was written for God's people. Psalm 53 speaks the same message for the people of every nation. God wanted people from every nation to know he was their God too!

This is a part of a larger pattern to Book Two of the Psalms. Yahweh (The Lord) is used more in Book One. Elohim is used more in Book Two. If Book One of the Psalms is more a songbook that speaks to Israel, Book Two is a songbook that tells people from every nation that the God of Israel is their God too! Salvation will come out of Israel, but it will be for everyone who believes in Jesus. More than half the psalms in Book Two speak about the "nations" and "peoples" of the earth and invites people from every tribe and language to obey God and give him praise.

A Closer Look

Read Psalm 14 and Psalm 53 together again.
What other differences do you see?

Psalm 58:4

King David's Victories
READ PSALMS 54–60

Psalms 54–60 describe seven of David's enemies and how he calls out for God. David knows he can't fight his enemies alone; he needs God's help. Whether we are young or old, we need God to protect us and help us when hard things happen. We might have to deal with sickness, trouble with family and friends, and we may also have a few enemies. When we run into troubles in life, we can turn back to these psalms for comfort and find our hope in God, just like David did.

Each of these songs ends by declaring God's victory over David's enemies. Even though David was afraid, he trusted God would save him. We know from history God answered David's prayers. Anytime you need God to help you in trouble you can pray one of these psalms in faith that God will also deliver you in your difficult times.

PSALM 54
God Protected David from Saul

Read the story in 1 Samuel 23:14–20.

David's Victory Praise:
"With a freewill offering I will sacrifice to you; I will give thanks to your name, O Lord, for it is good. For he has delivered me from every trouble, and my eye has looked in triumph on my enemies." (vv. 6–7)

Make a list of at least five things God has done for you in the past week and offer up a prayer of thanks to God for each item on your list.

PSALM 55
David's Son Absalom's Rebellion

Read the story in
2 Samuel 16:20—17:4.

David's Victory Praise:
"But you, O God, will cast them down into the pit of destruction; men of blood and treachery shall not live out half their days. But I will trust in you." (v. 23)

David begins this psalm asking God to hear his prayer. He knows God hears our prayers, but there is something about saying it that helps him (and us) to believe it. Start your prayer today with the first verse of Psalm 55 and then add your requests knowing God hears your prayers.

PSALM 56
David Escapes King Achish

Read the Story in
1 Samuel 21:10—22:1.

David's Victory Praise:
"For you have delivered my soul from death, yes, my feet from falling, that I may walk before God in the light of life." (v. 13)

When David was afraid, he put his trust in God. Make a list of your fears, then use verses 3–4 as a declaration of your faith in God. Pray and ask God to protect you and keep you safe from all your enemies and everything you are afraid of.

PSALM 57
David Spared the King

Read the story in
1 Samuel 24:1—7.

David's Victory Praise:
"They set a net for my steps; my soul was bowed down. They dug a pit in my way, but they have fallen into it themselves. . . . Be exalted, O God, above the heavens! Let your glory be over all the earth!" (vv. 6, 11)

David mixes prayer with praise all through this psalm. Take some time today to mix praise into your prayers. Ask God for what you need, but also praise God for who he is and the wonderful things he has done.

PSALM 58
Absalom's Lies

Read the story in
2 Samuel 15:1–6.

David's Victory Praise:
"Then people will say, 'Surely the righteous still are rewarded; surely there is a God who judges the earth.'" (v. 11 NIV)

Rather than take revenge on his enemies, David called out to God to deliver him and judge those who rose up against him. Ask God to deliver you from your enemies and trust your life to God's care and protection.

PSALM 59
Michal helps David Escape

Read the story in 1
Samuel 19:11–18.

David's Victory Praise:
"But I will sing of your strength; I will sing aloud of your steadfast love in the morning. For you have been to me a fortress and a refuge in the day of my distress. O my Strength, I will sing praises to you, for you, O God, are my fortress, the God who shows me steadfast love." (vv. 16–17)

After David shares his concerns and calls out to the Lord for help, he returns to faith-filled words at the end of this psalm and freshly dedicates his life to God. Share your prayer requests to God and then end your prayer time rededicating your life to God.

PSALM 60
David's Victories

Read the story in
2 Samuel 8:1–14.

David's Victory Praise:
"With God we shall do valiantly; it is he who will tread down our foes." (v. 12)

When we sin and turn from God like Israel did, God often allows and uses bad consequences to help us turn back to him. What are the bad consequences you have experienced from sinning against God in your life? How do they turn you back to God?

Psalm 68:1—3

How Faith Prays
READ PSALMS 61–68

Psalms 54–60 remember how God delivered David from his enemies. In Psalms 61–68 we see David's faith in God expressed. These psalms show us how we too can trust God during our trials.

When you find yourself in a struggle and your faith in God is weak, go back and read through David's battles with his enemies in Psalms 54–60 and then let the following faith-filled words from these psalms strengthen your trust in God and then use them to direct your prayers.

PSALM 61
Trust God as Your Refuge

"Hear my cry, O God, listen to my prayer; from the end of the earth I call to you when my heart is faint. Lead me to the rock that is higher than I, for you have been my refuge, a strong tower against the enemy. Let me dwell in your tent forever! Let me take refuge under the shelter of your wings!" (vv. 1–4)

The Psalms often reminds us that we can find safety from trouble by trusting in God. How is David feeling in this psalm? What does he remember about God that helps? What does he ask God for?

PSALM 62
Trust God for Your Salvation

"For God alone, O my soul, wait in silence, for my hope is from him. He only is my rock and my salvation, my fortress; I shall not be shaken. On God rests my salvation and my glory; my mighty rock, my refuge is God. Trust in him at all times, O people; pour out your heart before him; God is a refuge for us." (vv. 5–8)

David calls God his rock and fortress. How do you need God to be a rock and a fortress for you? Use your answer to create a prayer you can pray to ask for God's help.

PSALM 63
Trust God's Steadfast Love

"O God, you are my God; earnestly I seek you; my soul thirsts for you; my flesh faints for you, as in a dry and weary land where there is no water. So I have looked upon you in the sanctuary, beholding your power and glory. Because your steadfast love is better than life, my lips will praise you. So I will bless you as long as I live; in your name I will lift up my hands." (vv. 1—4)

When things are going well, it is easy to ignore God. One reason God allows trials is to remind us how much we need him. When you feel like you are in a dry and weary land, pray with David you will remember that God's love is better than life.

PSALM 64
Trust God to Protect You

"Hear me, my God, as I voice my complaint; protect my life from the threat of the enemy. Hide me from the conspiracy of the wicked, from the plots of evildoers." (vv. 1—2 NIV)

How can you apply David's prayer for God to protect him to your life? Do you have any enemies you need God to deliver you from? Remember that the world around us, our own self-centered desires, and the devil are common enemies to us all. Like David we can pray for protection from God. Don't forget Jesus conquered all of these enemies when he died and rose again.

PSALM 65
Remember God's Power

"You answer us with awesome and righteous deeds, God our Savior, the hope of all the ends of the earth and of the farthest seas, who formed the mountains by your power, having armed yourself with strength, who stilled the roaring of the seas, the roaring of their waves, and the turmoil of the nations. The whole earth is filled with awe at your wonders; where morning dawns, where evening fades, you call forth songs of joy." (vv. 5—8 NIV)

When you are worried, remind yourself like David did that God is all powerful. If he could create the world and all that is in it with a few simple commands, then he can help us with our problems. The whole earth is filled with awe at what God can do. We can trust such a powerful God with our troubles.

PSALM 66
Praise the Lord

"Shout for joy to God, all the earth; sing the glory of his name; give to him glorious praise! Say to God, 'How awesome are your deeds! So great is your power that your enemies come cringing to you. All the earth worships you and sings praises to you; they sing praises to your name.'" (vv. 1–4)

The Bible calls the whole earth to praise God. That means you don't have to be a Christian to praise God. Since everyone can see how awesome God's work in creation is, everyone should praise God. So, look around you and see the awesome things he's done and praise him!

PSALM 67
Ask for God's Blessing

"May God be gracious to us and bless us and make his face to shine upon us, that your way may be known on earth, your saving power among all nations. Let the peoples praise you, O God; let all the peoples praise you!" (vv. 1–3)

Psalm 67 is the high priest Aaron's blessing of Numbers 6:22–27 made into a song. It is meant to be prayed over God's people and sung by God's people. Use this blessing in your prayers this week to pray for your family and the church all over the world.

PSALM 68
Trust God to Judge Evil

"God shall arise, his enemies shall be scattered; and those who hate him shall flee before him! As smoke is driven away, so you shall drive them away; as wax melts before fire, so the wicked shall perish before God! But the righteous shall be glad; they shall exult before God; they shall be jubilant with joy!" (vv. 1–3)

God always wins in the end. While evil, hardship, and suffering are common, one day God is going to destroy them forever (Isaiah 25:8; Revelation 21:4). How does knowing this strengthen your faith to pray to God like David did for him to deliver us from evil?

The Suffering of Our Savior
READ PSALMS 69-71

Matthew 27:29

Did you know the Psalms can give you words to say to God when you are sad? The psalms that do this are called laments. A lament is an out loud cry of sorrow and grief. Have you ever done that? Psalms 69, 70, and 71 are all laments by King David. David wrote these songs about his life, but these psalms also point forward to Jesus. Jesus quoted Psalm 69:4 saying it is a prophetic word that he fulfilled (John 15:25). Other verses in Psalm 69

are quoted by John (John 19:28–29), Luke (Luke 23:36), and Paul (Romans 15:3) in the New Testament to describe the suffering of Jesus. Psalms 70 and 71 also point forward to Jesus and his suffering. As you read these psalms, notice how they connect to Jesus and also how they connect to your troubles.

PSALM 69

"More in number than the hairs of my head are those who hate me without cause; mighty are those who would destroy me, those who attack me with lies." (v. 4)

Connect it to Jesus:

Jesus quoted these words to describe himself in John 15:25.

"I have become a stranger to my brothers,
an alien to my mother's sons." (v.8)

Connect it to Jesus:

John 1:11 describes Jesus in the same way.

"For zeal for your house has consumed me,
and the reproaches of those who reproach you have
fallen on me." (v. 9)

Connect it to Jesus:

The disciples remembered the words of Psalm 69:9 as Jesus turned over the tables of the money-changers in the temple. John 2:17

"They gave me poison for food, and for my thirst they gave me sour wine to drink." (v. 21)

Connect it to Jesus:

The soldiers offered Jesus sour wine (John 19:29) and wine mixed with a poison called gall (Matthew 27:34).

Connect it to you:

Take time to thank God for the way the Psalms point forward to Jesus and encourage us with the prophecies that were written ages before Jesus was ever born. How does knowing God is in control of all things help strengthen you? Then read this psalm again thinking about your troubles. What are some ways David describes to God how he is feeling? What does David ask God to do for him? You can pray in this same way when you are experiencing trouble.

PSALM 70

"Let them be put to shame and confusion who seek my life! Let them be turned back and brought to dishonor who delight in my hurt! Let them turn back because of their shame who say, 'Aha, Aha!'" (vv. 2–3)

Connect it to Jesus:

The people who made fun of Jesus on the cross used the word "Aha" to mock him. (Mark 15:29)

Connect it to you:

No help came to Jesus when he cried out to the Father (Matthew 27:36). God the Father abandoned his Son and punished him for our sin. But then something amazing happened. Death could not hold the perfect Son of God. Jesus rose from the dead and now he lives forever! Reread Psalm 70 and think of Jesus in verses 1–3, but remember that today we can rejoice with Jesus that he is alive, ruling the universe with all power. On the cross Jesus defeated our biggest enemies—sin, death, and Satan. Now you can be sure that verses 4–5 will be true for you and all who trust in Jesus. Make them your own prayer to God.

PSALM 71

"For my enemies speak concerning me; those who watch for my life consult together and say, 'God has forsaken him; pursue and seize him, for there is none to deliver him.'" (vv. 10–11)

Connect it to Jesus:

People mocked Jesus saying, "He trusts in God; let God deliver him now, if he desires him. For he said, 'I am the Son of God.' And the robbers who were crucified with him also reviled him in the same way." (Matthew 27:43–44).

Connect it to you:

In this psalm, David asks God to "be to me a rock of refuge, to which I may continually come; you have given the command to save me, for you are my rock and fortress" (v. 3). When you are in trouble, you can remember who God is and how he will protect and help you. That's how to pray by faith in God when you are in a hard time. The Psalms are full of faith-filled prayers. Ask God to give you faith so you can trust in him like the psalm writers did.

The Perfect King
READ PSALM 72

Give the king your justice, O God,
    and your righteousness to the royal son! (v. 1)

David is near the end of his life and will soon meet Jesus face-to-face. As he looks back over his years as king—he also looks *ahead* to his son, Solomon, taking his place. Psalm 72 is David's prayer over his son.

Looking back, we can see how God answered David's prayers. David prayed that his son would rule from sea to sea. Solomon ruled all the land, and the kings of the earth bowed before Solomon and gave him gifts of gold—just as David prayed.

Solomon began as a good and wise king, but he made some foolish mistakes. He turned away from God. In the end he loved what he had in this world—his wives, his things, and his gold—more than God. But there is a perfect King who didn't turn away and make the mistakes Solomon did. Jesus is that perfect King! He always obeyed his Father and never turned to evil. He came to defeat sin, death, and evil. Jesus rules all the earth, and one day every knee will bow before him and know that he is God. He is unbeatable and unmatchable. There is none like him!

Think about the day when Jesus will reign on earth as the King of all kings. Imagine what it will be like. Are you excited? Why are you thankful for a King like Jesus?

A Closer Look

Reread Psalm 72 and pay special attention to what the psalm says are the characteristics of a good king. Then, write a prayer, thanking Jesus for being all these things for us. He is the perfect and eternal King.

Chapter Three

Oliver's Story:

Oliver Reads to Grandpa

The leafy branches and dense shade of the old oak were no match for the mid-August heat. Grandpa took out his handkerchief and wiped his face. "Tomorrow we will begin Book Three."

"Thank you for meeting with me each day, Grandpa. I never knew how much I'd learn about Jesus through the Psalms."

"One day we will sing these songs in heaven, along with the angels!" Grandpa wiped his brow and sighed.

"Is it hard for you to walk out here to the oak tree?" Oliver asked. Over the last few weeks, Grandpa's appearance had changed. He was thinner, and his face was lined with more wrinkles. He looked tired.

"I'm holding up," Grandpa answered. "I just move slower in the heat." Grandpa paused, then continued, "Soon the leaves will change and the acorns will fall. I remember reading these same stories to your dad under the fallen leaves."

"You read these to my dad?"

"Yes, I read to your father under these same trees. Your dad planned to read this book to you this summer. He asked me to send it for your birthday, but God had a different plan. When your father asked if he could move your family in with me, I said yes on one condition—that I could read the book with you myself. Oliver, I knew that things were not going well for you, and I prayed the Lord would grant this last request: to share his amazing words with you. I knew you loved to read, but I wasn't sure you'd be interested in me reading with you. But, I took that up with the Lord and he answered."

Oliver hugged his grandfather and prayed silently, *God, help me pass on your words to others, just like Grandpa has done with me.*

"I'll tell you what, Oliver," Grandpa said, shifting his weight, which was the signal it was time to head back to the house. "Tomorrow, I want *you* to start reading to *me*. That will give you the practice you are going to need in sharing this message with others." It was as though Grandpa read his mind.

"Sure, Grandpa," Oliver answered. He stood, offered his hand to his grandfather, and helped pull him to his feet.

Book

Nº 3

Psalms 73–89

THE SONGS OF ASAPH

God Is All I Need
READ PSALM 73

But as for me, my feet had almost stumbled,
  my steps had nearly slipped.
For I was envious of the arrogant
  when I saw the prosperity of the wicked.
(vv. 2–3)

Have you ever seen a friend with a cool toy, game, or device and wish you could have it for your own? When others have things we don't have, it can lead us to be sad about our lives. We can even question God and wonder if he is really good.

That is what happened to Asaph, and he tells us about it in Psalm 73 to help us see God is all we need. Asaph saw the riches of the people who did not love God and his heart became bitter against God. He was mad God did not give him the same wealth and blessing he saw others had.

But the Holy Spirit helped Asaph to see God was all he needed. We see at the end of this psalm where Asaph tells us there is nothing he desires more than God. Think about it. God watches over us and guides us every day. He gives us everything we need like food, drink, clothes to wear, and he keeps our heart beating all by itself. The earthly things we long for will all one day fall apart. But God, the best treasure of all, will be with those who love him forever.

Whenever we feel sad because someone has something we don't have, let's remember what Asaph said about God—that God is all we need. "My flesh and my heart may fail, but God is the strength of my heart and my portion forever" (v. 26).

A Closer Look

Read verses 23–28 again. Now rewrite them as your prayer to remind yourself of all the things God does for you that can never be taken away.

Remember
READ PSALM 74

Yet God my King is from of old,
working salvation in the midst of the earth.
(v. 12)

Have you ever had a good friend move away? You promise you will always be friends, but as times passes, you're not as close as you used to be. Sometimes you have to remind yourself of what he or she was like. The longer they're gone, the harder it becomes.

In today's psalm, the Israelites are trying to remember God. They haven't seen him in a while, and he feels far away. They no longer receive signs from him, and all the prophets have moved to other towns.

When the Israelites refused to turn from their sin, they were destroyed by another nation, called Babylon. As a result, they lost their temple and all of their belongings. Now, they are looking back on all that's happened and turning to God for help. They are searching for God and hoping to find him. They cry out: Please don't forget us! Remember we are your chosen people. Please help us!

The Israelites have hope because they remember God's power—that he is the only God who can save. He chose them and rescued them from slavery and opened the Red Sea so they could escape Egypt's army. He gave them signs and miracles. They've seen his power and know what he can do. So, they choose to remember him and depend on his deliverance.

We also need to remember God's faithfulness to us. How has he helped you in the past? Think back on his faithfulness, and trust that he will be your Helper again.

A Closer Look

Make a list of all the things the Israelites remembered about
God's faithfulness and help (starting with verse 12). Then make a list
of some of the ways God has helped you and people you know.
If you can't think of any, ask your parents to remind you.

The King of All Kings
READ PSALMS 75–77

While Psalms 74 and 79 speak of the destruction of God's city, the three psalms in between (75–77) remind us that God is in control. These psalms describe God's rule and power over the kings of the earth. The Bible tells us God is king over history, and all things follow his plan (2 Chronicles 20:6, Ephesians 1:11). Even evil deeds are used by God for good. God tells us through the prophets that he used the Babylonians to judge the sin of his people (Habakkuk 1:5–6). Since God is in control, we don't have to worry in times of trouble, even when our enemies attack us.

We learned from David in Psalm 22 that kingship belongs to the Lord, and he rules over the nations (Psalm 22:28). Solomon teaches "The king's heart is a stream of water in the hand of the Lord; he turns it wherever he will" (Proverbs 21:1).

Psalm 75 reminds us it is God who lifts one ruler up and puts down another. Psalm 76 tells us God rules in judgment over the kings of the earth. The writer of Psalm 77 calls us to pray and cry out to God and remember his mighty deeds and meditate on them. We can know God is with us through our trouble, even when it doesn't seem like God is there.

PSALM 75
God Rules over All

"When the earth totters, and all its inhabitants, it is I who keep steady its pillars." (v. 3)

Psalm 75 teaches us about God's power and control over all things. Which verses of this psalm are most encouraging to you? Do you know anyone who might be encouraged if you shared this psalm with them?

PSALM 76
God Saves the Humble

"From the heavens you uttered judgment; the earth feared and was still, when God arose to establish judgment, to save all the humble of the earth. . . . Make your vows to the Lord your God and perform them; let all around him bring gifts to him who is to be feared, who cuts off the spirit of princes, who is to be feared by the kings of the earth." (vv. 8–9, 11–12)

Proverbs teach us that the truly wise are those who trust God and worship him. The Bible calls that "the fear of the Lord" (Proverbs 9:10). That's what it means to be humble. When we know how powerful God is and that he saves the humble, that can help us to say "no" to sin and follow God.

PSALM 77
God's Saves Us When We Are in Trouble

"I cry aloud to God, aloud to God, and he will hear me. In the day of my trouble I seek the Lord."
"Your way was through the sea, your path through the great waters; yet your footprints were unseen. You led your people like a flock by the hand of Moses and Aaron." (vv. 1–2, 19–20)

Notice how honest Asaph is as he shares his prayer with God. The next time you are going through a time of trouble, uses Asaph's lament as a guide to form your own lament to God and ask him for help to get you through.

It is I who keep steady its pillars.

Psalm 75:3

A Closer Look

Just as God worked wonders in the Bible, he is continually working wonders in your life and in the world around you. Who might be encouraged by God's story? Maybe someone at school or in your neighborhood? Think of one or two friends (or family members) you could share God's story with. God wants his wonders to spread like wildfire across the world, and you can be part of it!

Tell of His Wonders
READ PSALM 78

We will not hide them from their children,
 but tell to the coming generation
the glorious deeds of the LORD, and his might,
 and the wonders that he has done. (v. 4)

Imagine you just got home from an amazing family vacation. You have a new mug, photos, and incredible stories to share. You can't wait to see your friends and tell them all about it! In today's psalm, Asaph feels the same way, and he can't *wait* to share an exciting story!

The story Asaph wants to tell is God's story—the greatest story ever written! He wants everyone to know and remember all that God did. Most important, Asaph wants to be sure all the children in Israel hear about God. Asaph knows that one day the children of Israel will grow up and have children of their own. Then they can pass the story of God on to them. Then those kids will grow up to tell their children too!

Have you ever shared God's story with others? Have you shared the good news that Jesus came to rescue sinners? Are you excited to share the wonder of his story with others?

Take a moment to consider some things God has done in your life. Where have you seen his power? How have you sensed him near? Do you have a story of God's faithfulness to share?

God's story is the best story on earth—one of power and joy. Tell of his wonders today.

Our Trouble and God's Help
READ PSALMS 79-83

The last five psalms of Asaph speak of the future trouble and bad consequences that come upon God's people when they turn away from him. But these songs also have prayers of hope—hope that God would help his people and deliver them from their enemies. Like the other psalms with Asaph's name, we see his passion for God in the midst of the trouble. We also again hear Asaph's desire for the future generations of God's children to praise the Lord. Asaph writes, "We your people, the sheep of your pasture, will give thanks to you forever; from generation to generation we will recount your praise" (Psalm 79:13).

These psalms are asking God to deliver Israel from the nations, but they also point to a greater need— our need to be rescued from sin. Jesus, the "son of man" (Psalm 80:17), gave up his life to pay the penalty we deserved to "atone" (Psalm 79:9) for our sins. Our sinful hearts want us to believe that our sins are not such a big deal. But God's Word teaches us that any sin can get us into big time trouble. That is why we should confess our sins to God and ask him to forgive us and lead us away from temptations (Matthew 6:13).

PSALM 79
Only God Can Atone for Our Sins

Our Trouble

"O God, the nations have come into your inheritance; they have defiled your holy temple; they have laid Jerusalem in ruins." (v. 1)

God's Help

"Help us, O God of our salvation, for the glory of your name; deliver us, and atone for our sins, for your name's sake!" (v. 9)

We can't fight sin without God's help. Using verse 9 of this psalm as your guide, pray and ask God to deliver you (rescue you) from your sins.

PSALM 80
Only God Can Save Us

Our Trouble

"You transplanted a vine from Egypt; you drove out the nations and planted it. You cleared the ground for it, and it took root and filled the land. The mountains were covered with its shade, the mighty cedars with its branches. Its branches reached as far as the Sea, its shoots as far as the River. Why have you broken down its walls so that all who pass by pick its grapes? Boars from the forest ravage it, and insects from the fields feed on it." (vv. 8–13 NIV)

God's Help

"Return to us, God Almighty! Look down from heaven and see! Watch over this vine, the root your right hand has planted, the son you have raised up for yourself. Your vine is cut down, it is burned with fire; at your rebuke your people perish. Let your hand rest on the man at your right hand, the son of man you have raised up for yourself. Then we will not turn away from you; revive us, and we will call on your name. Restore us, Lord God Almighty; make your face shine on us, that we may be saved." (vv. 14–19 NIV)

Psalm 80 is a prayer for Israel, the people of God. Today, all those who put their hope and faith in Jesus are a part of God's people, the church of God. Read Psalm 80 looking for verses that apply to all those who believe in God. Then use them to pray for the church.

PSALM 81
Only God Can Defeat Our Enemies

Our Trouble

"I am the Lord your God, who brought you up out of the land of Egypt. Open your mouth wide, and I will fill it. 'But my people did not listen to my voice; Israel would not submit to me. So I gave them over to their stubborn hearts, to follow their own counsels.'" (vv. 10–12)

God's Help

"Oh, that my people would listen to me, that Israel would walk in my ways! I would soon subdue their enemies and turn my hand against their foes." (vv. 13–14)

When Israel turned away from God, he allowed the bad consequences of their sin to fall on them (see verses 11–15). Ask God to help you walk in his ways. Isn't it wonderful that because of Jesus we know God forgives us when we say we are sorry for turning away from him? Ask God to give you a heart that wants to follow his ways.

PSALM 82
Only God Can Deliver Us

Our Trouble

"God has taken his place in the divine council; in the midst of the gods he holds judgment: 'How long will you judge unjustly and show partiality to the wicked? Give justice to the weak and the fatherless; maintain the right of the afflicted and the destitute.'" (vv. 1–3)

God's Help

"Rescue the weak and the needy; deliver them from the hand of the wicked." (v. 4)

God is a just judge. Whenever we see injustice in the world we can pray to God and ask him to rescue the poor and needy or help the fatherless and the widow. Create your own prayer to God and ask him to rescue a person or group of people.

PSALM 83
Only God Can Help Us

Our Trouble

"O God, do not keep silence; do not hold your peace or be still, O God! For behold, your enemies make an uproar; those who hate you have raised their heads. They lay crafty plans against your people; they consult together against your treasured ones. They say, 'Come, let us wipe them out as a nation; let the name of Israel be remembered no more!'" (vv. 1–4)

God's Help

"O my God, make them like whirling dust, like chaff before the wind. As fire consumes the forest, as the flame sets the mountains ablaze, so may you pursue them with your tempest and terrify them with your hurricane!" (vv. 13–15)

Asaph is asking God to destroy the enemies of God's people. Did you know that behind all the enemies of God's people stands the devil? He wants to destroy the faith of all who trust in Jesus. We can pray that God will protect our faith and destroy Satan. Pray also for persecuted believers around the world. Pray that those who are persecuting them would turn to Christ. It's happened before!

Rescue the weak and the needy;

deliver them from the hand of the wicked.

Psalm 82:4

Prayers for Times of Trouble
READ PSALMS 84-88

After the five psalms that describe the rebellion of God's people and the trouble that came to them, the editor of Psalms places five psalms we can pray to God in times of trouble. While some of these psalms call us to lift our eyes to the Lord and focus on heaven, others, like Psalm 88, teach us to share our sorrows with God honestly and ask him for help.

When you go through times of trouble, remember to turn to these psalms to help you guide your prayers. Through reading the Psalms we learn how to talk to God about our troubles, how to rest in God's promises, and to remember his blessings.

PSALM 84
Rest in God's Presence

"For a day in your courts is better than a thousand elsewhere. I would rather be a doorkeeper in the house of my God than dwell in the tents of the wicked. For the LORD God is a sun and shield; the LORD bestows favor and honor. No good thing does he withhold from those who walk uprightly. O LORD of hosts, blessed is the one who trusts in you!" (vv. 10–12)

One day in God's court (in his presence) is greater than a thousand days far from God (v. 10). God promises to send his Holy Spirit (Luke 11:13) to live with believers every day! Ask God to help you put your trust in Jesus and ask him to fill you with his Spirit.

PSALM 85
Ask for God to Revive You and Speak Peace to You

"Will you not revive us again, that your people may rejoice in you? Show us your steadfast love, O LORD, and grant us your salvation. Let me hear what God the LORD will speak, for he will speak peace to his people, to his saints; but let them not turn back to folly. Surely his salvation is near to those who fear him, that glory may dwell in our land." (vv. 6–9)

In times of trouble it can feel like our faith and hope are dying. Ask God to revive you. Remembering his steadfast love will speak peace to your heart. The Psalms encourage us to remember the faithfulness of God again and again. Today take a moment to remember what God has done for you and your family. Then ask God for help in your time of need.

PSALM 86
Ask for God's Help and Declare God's Praises

"Incline your ear, O Lord, and answer me, for I am poor and needy. Preserve my life, for I am godly; save your servant, who trusts in you—you are my God. Be gracious to me, O Lord, for to you do I cry all the day. Gladden the soul of your servant, for to you, O Lord, do I lift up my soul." (vv. 1–4)

"There is none like you among the gods, O Lord, nor are there any works like yours. All the nations you have made shall come and worship before you, O Lord, and shall glorify your name. For you are great and do wondrous things; you alone are God. Teach me your way, O Lord, that I may walk in your truth; unite my heart to fear your name." (vv. 8–11)

When life is full of trouble, we feel poor and needy. Ask God to help you with all your troubles. God hears your cry for help and he will answer you. Read this psalm and make a list of all the things the writer says about who God is that help him trust God in hard times.

Use this psalm to guide your prayers. First present your requests, then praise and thank God as a way to show you believe in him and trust him to deliver you.

PSALM 87
Remember God's Blessings

"On the holy mount stands the city he founded; the Lord loves the gates of Zion more than all the dwelling places of Jacob." (vv. 1–2)

Once again the psalmist reminds himself and us of what God has done and praises him for those things. What has God done for you that you can praise him for? Offer God a short prayer of praise and thankfulness for all he has done.

PSALM 88
Honestly Tell God Your Troubles

"O Lord, God of my salvation, I cry out day and night before you. Let my prayer come before you; incline your ear to my cry! For my soul is full of troubles, and my life draws near to Sheol. I am counted among those who go down to the pit. I am a man who has no strength. " (vv. 1–4)

"But I, O Lord, cry to you; in the morning my prayer comes before you. O Lord, why do you cast my soul away? Why do you hide your face from me?" (vv. 13–14)

God wants us to share our troubles honestly. That's one reason he gave us these psalms, so we know it is okay to tell him exactly how we are feeling. If you are in the middle of a struggle, tell God how hard it is. Circle Psalm 88 in your Bible and come back to it as a guide to help you know how to pray during a trial or challenge.

A Kingdom That Lasts Forever
READ PSALM 89

"You have said, 'I have made a covenant with my chosen one;
   I have sworn to David my servant:
'I will establish your offspring forever,
   and build your throne for all generations.'" (vv. 3–4)

Today's psalm is written by a wise man named Ethan. He lived in the time of King David and Solomon. He saw David rule as king, and he saw Solomon take the throne. He watched as so much changed in his world.

Ethan begins by remembering God's promise to David—that his kingdom would last forever. Ethan has to work hard to remember this promise because everything has changed so much. Solomon has turned away from the Lord, and so has his son. Israel doesn't look like God's nation anymore. So Ethan asks God, "Where is your steadfast love?" (v. 49). He wonders if God's promise is still true.

As Ethan watches the world around him falling apart, he chooses to trust God's promise. His prayer looks ahead to the day when Jesus will rule as the only perfect King. His throne will last forever and all of his promises will come true.

As you look at the world around you, do you sometimes feel like Ethan? Do you wonder when God will make all things right? Do you wonder if he'll keep his promises? Follow Ethan's example in trusting God's promises to be true, and look forward to the day when Jesus will return. When he comes, he will destroy all evil, sin, and death and reign forever in truth and power!

A Closer Look

Read the psalm again. This time, when you get to verse 18 substitute the word *Jesus* for *Lord* and *him*. You will see how the psalm becomes a praise to Jesus and a fulfilment of Ethan's prayer.

Chapter Four

Oliver's Story:

God Is the Strength of Grandpa's Heart

Grandpa smiled at Oliver from his bed, as the winter wind howled outside, and the sleet danced on the rooftop.

"Well, that's the end of Book Three, Grandpa," Oliver said, closing the book.

"Thank you, Oliver. You did an excellent job. I'm thankful to be back home reading again. You didn't read ahead while I was in the hospital, did you?"

"No, I waited just like I promised." Oliver smiled.

Mom entered the room with a tray of steaming mugs. She said, "Who's ready for some hot chocolate?" She set the tray on the side table.

"That sounds wonderful. Thank you," said Grandpa.

The wind drove another icy blast against the window, drawing Oliver's attention. He remembered the first morning at the farm, looking at the summer landscape out this same window. So much had changed in so little time—with the seasons changing and with Grandpa. Mom set her hand on Oliver's shoulder. She seemed to know what he was thinking. She assured him with her presence that all would be okay.

"Grandpa, do you think the oak will make it through the storm?" asked Oliver.

"It will be just fine and likely live another hundred years. Besides, have you seen what's growing along the path, at the base of the old poplar?"

Oliver didn't remember seeing anything. "What is it?" he asked.

"I meant to show you! At least half a dozen acorns sprouted last spring. Although the squirrels try to bury as many acorns as they can, they often forget some of their hiding places. Those acorns sit dormant through the winter and then sprout in the spring.

"Many years before the passing of the old oak, those saplings will rise and stand beside it. They will provide food and shelter for the animals. They might even shade future readers, like us." Grandpa smiled.

Oliver said, "You'll have to show me in the spring."

"I'm not sure I'll make it there again. I sense that it's nearly time for me to go home. Your dad has already agreed to take my place and read with you. 'Whom have I in heaven but you? And there is nothing on earth that I desire besides you. My flesh and my heart may fail, but God is the strength of my heart and my portion forever.'"

Oliver whispered, "Psalm 73."

Grandpa smiled and thought: *Oliver will always remember the Psalms. They will guide his thoughts and prayers. Thank you, Father.*

Book
Nº 4

Psalms 90–106

THE LORD IS KING

God's True Story
READ PSALM 90

Lord, you have been our dwelling place
    in all generations.
Before the mountains were brought forth,
    or ever you had formed the earth and the world,
    from everlasting to everlasting you are God. (vv. 1–2)

Can you remember all the Christmas presents and birthday presents your parents and grandparents got for you? Imagine them all piled up in one big pile. Through the years we receive a lot of great gifts, but it is easy to forget those blessings when we have a bad day.

Today's psalm was written by Moses. He is very aware of all the trouble Israel has endured. He and God's people have been wandering in the desert for forty years. In times of trouble it's easy to forget God's true story and to just think about the trouble we are facing. Maybe you are facing trouble in your family, at school, or in your neighborhood. All you can see is what is in front of you, and you're having trouble remembering God's help in the past.

Remind yourself of God's true story—both in the Bible and in your own life. Think back on God's faithfulness throughout Scripture, and his faithfulness to you. Then ask God to fill you with hope and trust, no matter what new troubles arise. Spend time reading his Word. It never changes. He is the same God yesterday, today, and forever. His story is true and trustworthy. That's what it means to "number our days that we may get a heart of wisdom" (v. 12). When we know God is in charge of every day and that every day is a day to trust in his steadfast love, then we are on the road to wisdom.

A Closer Look

Write down all the things Moses says happens to everyone who lives on this earth (see vv. 3–10). Then write down all the things Moses remembers about God. How does that change the way you look at your life?

A Closer Look

Make a list from this psalm of all the images that help us to remember how God keeps us safe.

My Safe Place
READ PSALM 91

He who dwells in the shelter of the Most High
 will abide in the shadow of the Almighty.
I will say to the Lord, "My refuge and my fortress,
 my God, in whom I trust." (vv. 1–2)

Have you ever woken in the middle of the night from a bad dream? Suddenly everything in your bedroom looks different. Everything *sounds* different too! You need help—and fast! Where can you go? Do you call out for help? Doesn't it feel good when your mom or dad or brother or sister rush in and give you a hug and say, "You're okay. It was only a bad dream."

In today's psalm, David shares that God is the one he calls out to for help. David says God is like a fortress he can run to and be safe. Nothing harmful or scary can touch him there. He is covered by God's wings and hides under his feathers. David finds his safety in God. Psalm 91 holds a promise for all of us—that God will guard all those who take refuge in him. A refuge is a safe place to hide for protection, like a shelter from a storm. The message of Psalm 91 is if we place our trust in God he will save us.

Have you, like David, found God to be your safe place and refuge? Can you turn to him when you are scared? Because of God's faithful love and care, you no longer need to fear the shadows of night, or the surprises of the day. God is with you always. He will protect you. He is your safe place. You can rest.

Today, take time to share your fears with God. He is listening and will answer. When you are in trouble, he will surround you with his love.

Worship in the Psalms
READ PSALM 92

It is good to give thanks to the LORD,
    to sing praises to your name, O Most High; . . .
For you, O LORD, have made me glad by your work;
    at the works of your hands I sing for joy. (vv. 1, 4)

Take a moment and think about all that God has done. God created the earth and the heavens above with all the planets and stars. He filled the earth with wonderful animals like ladybugs, bluebirds, and butterflies. God also takes care of us. The Bible is filled with stories of God saving his people from trouble, healing their diseases, and answering their prayers.

One of the ways we can worship God is to praise and give thanks to him for his wonderful works. Psalm 92 says it is *good* to praise God. It's good to praise him on Sunday at church, and it's good to praise him at home. It's good to praise him with others or on your own. It's good to praise him anywhere and at any time!

Today's psalm says you can sing of God's love in the morning and of his faithfulness at night. You can praise him at any time of the day! You can lift your heart to God in praise through prayer and songs. God loves to hear the praise of your heart as you lift high his name! He loves to hear your heart sing.

How can you praise God today? What has he done for you? Shout out a thank-you to God. Shout out things like, "Thank you, God, for my family! Thank you, God, for keeping my heart beating. Thank you for the clouds in the sky and the sun that shines!" You can tell others or simply talk to God in the quiet of your room—sharing your heart and offering praise. Whatever you do, lift your heart to God. Declare his glory! Sing praises to his name. It's good to give thanks for the Lord!

A Closer Look

Write down one amazing thing you would like to praise God for today. Then take a few moments to praise God by writing a poem, singing a song, or saying a prayer.

The Lord Is Our King
READ PSALMS 93–99

Psalms 93–99 are full of reasons to praise our God as King. Together they are meant to stir our hearts to shout and sing, "My God is my King! My God is my King! He rules over my troubles! His praises I sing!"

Kings can do evil or good. When the people of a country have a good king, they shout and clap when he appears from his castle to speak. God, our heavenly King who rules over all, is perfect and good in all he does. That is why we shout, and clap, and sing his praises!

These psalms contain the Hebrew praise, *Yahweh Malak*, which means "The LORD reigns as King" and is translated, "the LORD reigns" (Psalm 93:1; 96:10; 97:1; 99:1). This collection of psalms call us to "sing" praises to the King and rejoice over God (Psalm 95:1; 96:1–2; 96:12; 98:4–5; 98:8; 100:2). As you read through these psalms, look for these two themes and join in the rejoicing. Our Lord reigns as King, so let us lift our voices loud and sing for all the reasons we are given to praise our King!

PSALM 93
Praise Our King Who Is Eternal

"The LORD reigns; he is robed in majesty; the LORD is robed; he has put on strength as his belt. Yes, the world is established; it shall never be moved. Your throne is established from of old; you are from everlasting. (vv. 1–2)

We can use the descriptions of God in the Psalms to praise him as we pray. Keep in mind that God is your King as you read through this psalm and offer up each line as a prayer.

PSALM 94
Praise Our King Who Is Just

"O LORD, God of vengeance, O God of vengeance, shine forth! Rise up, O judge of the earth; repay to the proud what they deserve!" (vv. 1–2)

This psalm praises God for his justice, but the psalmist is also honest with God and asks God why his justice is taking so long. We don't always understand why God allows evil to continue. It's good to share our questions with God in our prayers. Do you have any questions you would like to ask him?

The
LORD
reigns;

he is robed in majesty. . . .

Psalm 93:1

PSALM 95
Praise Our King Who Is Higher than All

"Oh come, let us sing to the LORD; let us make a joyful noise to the rock of our salvation! Let us come into his presence with thanksgiving; let us make a joyful noise to him with songs of praise! For the LORD is a great God, and a great King above all gods." (vv. 1–3)

The Psalms were sung by God's people in days of old. Do you have a favorite hymn or praise song you can sing today? Think about the words you sing and make them your personal prayer.

PSALM 96
Praise Our King Who Is Righteous and Faithful

"Say among the nations, 'The LORD reigns! Yes, the world is established; it shall never be moved; he will judge the peoples with equity.' Let the heavens be glad, and let the earth rejoice; let the sea roar, and all that fills it; let the field exult, and everything in it! Then shall all the trees of the forest sing for joy before the LORD, for he comes, for he comes to judge the earth. He will judge the world in righteousness, and the peoples in his faithfulness." (vv. 10–13)

Here is something fun to try: turn your prayers into a new song by making up your own melody. Don't worry if your song isn't that great; God loves to hear his people sing and will love it anyway.

PSALM 97
Praise Our King Who Is Powerful

"The LORD reigns, let the earth rejoice; let the many coastlands be glad! Clouds and thick darkness are all around him; righteousness and justice are the foundation of his throne. Fire goes before him and burns up his adversaries all around. His lightnings light up the world; the earth sees and trembles. The mountains melt like wax before the LORD, before the Lord of all the earth." (vv. 1–5)

Thinking about God as the all-powerful King who rules over all of his creation builds our faith. Read through the words of Psalm 97 slowly and as you go through each line, pray that you will believe every word of this psalm. Trust God as your great King.

PSALM 98
Praise Our King Who Is Lord over All

"Make a joyful noise to the LORD, all the earth; break forth into joyous song and sing praises! Sing praises to the LORD with the lyre, with the lyre and the sound of melody! With trumpets and the sound of the horn make a joyful noise before the King, the LORD!" (vv. 4–6)

The Psalms call us to sing to God and praise him. While you might think, I've already done that before, singing is meant to be a regular part of our lives as believers. Sing at church, sing with your family, and sing in private too. God loves for us to sing praises to him.

PSALM 99
Praise Our King Who Is Holy

"The LORD reigns; let the peoples tremble! He sits enthroned upon the cherubim; let the earth quake! The LORD is great in Zion; he is exalted over all the peoples. Let them praise your great and awesome name! Holy is he! The King in his might loves justice. You have established equity; you have executed justice and righteousness in Jacob. Exalt the LORD our God; worship at his footstool! Holy is he!" (vv. 1–5)

The Psalms are filled with references to past history and the things God has done. What has God done for you? Make up your own psalm describing God's work in your life, then pray it back to God and thank him.

let us
sing
to
the LORD;

let us make a joyful noise
to the rock of our salvation!

Psalm 95

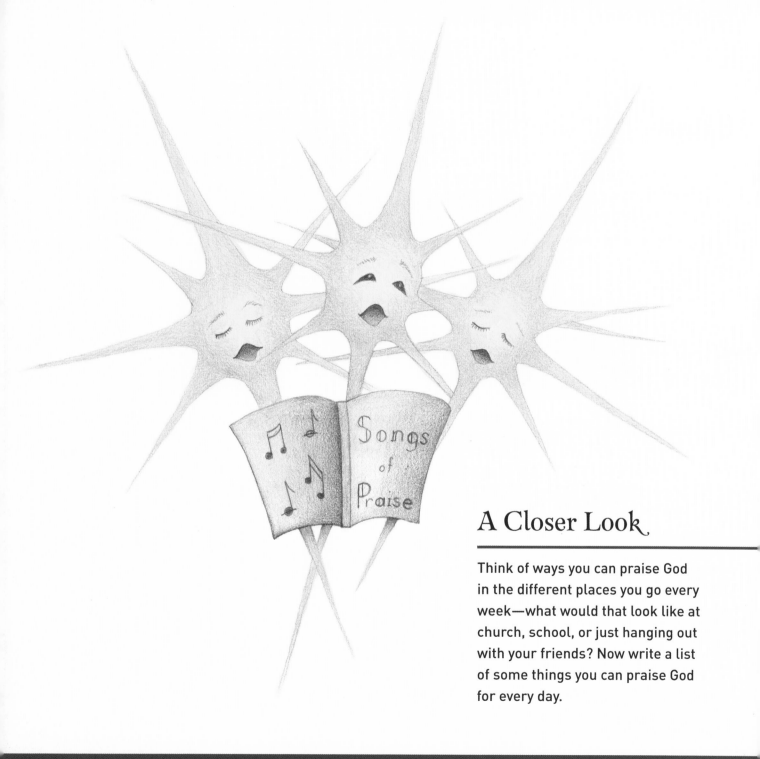

A Closer Look

Think of ways you can praise God in the different places you go every week—what would that look like at church, school, or just hanging out with your friends? Now write a list of some things you can praise God for every day.

Praise God Everywhere You Are
READ PSALM 100

Make a joyful noise to the LORD, all the earth! Serve
the LORD with gladness!
    Come into his presence with singing!
Know that the LORD, he is God!
    It is he who made us, and we are his;
    we are his people, and the sheep of his pasture. (vv. 1–3)

This psalm tells the whole earth to make a joyful noise to praise God. Did you know God says even the morning stars sang when the world was created (Job 38:7)? Can you imagine hearing that? We have so many things to praise God for. Can you think of some? This psalm tells us the most important reasons we have to praise the Lord—he is God of the whole world, he made us, and he takes care of us. His love lasts forever. That's something to shout for joy about!

When this psalm was written, the temple was the place in Jerusalem where God's people went to meet with him. When Jesus began his ministry, he said he was the temple (John 2:21). Jesus is our Emmanuel—God with us. Before he went to heaven, Jesus promised to send the Holy Spirit to live in the heart of everyone who believes so God could be with each one of us (John 14:17).

That makes everyone who believes in Jesus a part of God's living temple (1 Corinthians 3:16). God's Spirit lives in us, so we can make a joyful noise to God everywhere we go. We can praise him at church, at home, in school, or any place at all.

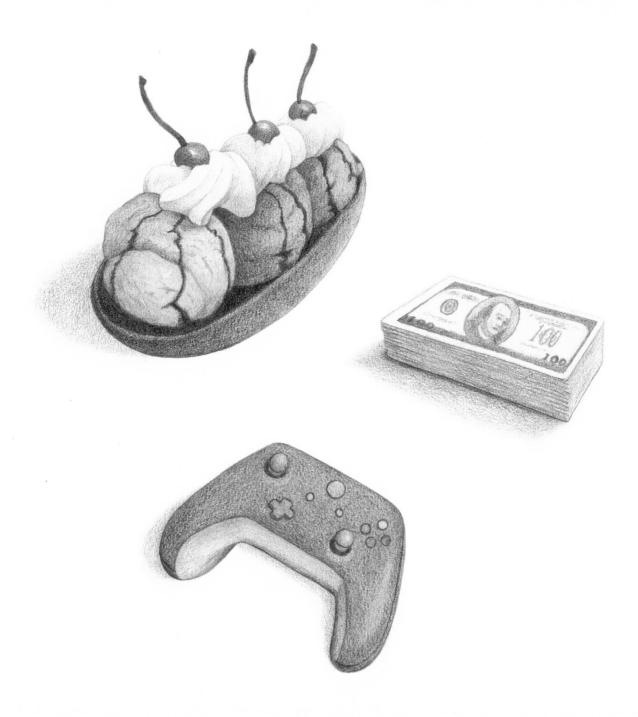

David's Promise
READ PSALM 101

I will walk with integrity of heart
    within my house;
I will not set before my eyes
    anything that is worthless. (vv. 2–3)

King David knew life was filled with good things that could steal our love from God. What are some good things you love? Perhaps it's food or having fun with your friends or watching a show. It's wonderful to enjoy all the good things God gives us, but when you love them more than God they are what King David calls "worthless." In today's psalm, David makes a promise to God. He promises to love God with his entire life—with every thought and action. That's what it means to have integrity. But before he can keep this promise, he needs God's help. That's why King David says to God, "When will you come to me?" He knows he can only love God with his whole heart if Jesus is with him. You can make that promise today too. But you also will need Jesus to be with you every step of the way. Ask him to come to you and he will. Jesus says when we ask, seek, and knock, he will always answer with his presence (Matthew 7:7).

Because Jesus is with us, we can make David's pledge our prayer. Look through the verses. Which of these lines do you think the Holy Spirit wants you to make as a promise to God? One of the most helpful promises in King David's song is found in verse 3, "I will not set before my eyes anything that is worthless." That is a great reminder for us to guard our eyes from seeing images that don't honor God.

A Closer Look

What might be some good things in your life that you spend more time thinking about than God? Ask God to help you put him first in your heart and then thank him for all the wonderful blessings he has given you.

Difficult Days
READ PSALM 102

Hear my prayer, O Lord;
     let my cry come to you!
Do not hide your face from me
     in the day of my distress!
Incline your ear to me;
     answer me speedily in the day when I call!
(vv. 1–2)

Have you ever had a difficult day? It can feel as if the entire world is against you—as if a storm cloud is hovering over your head, just waiting to rain upon you. No matter where you go or what you do, you can't seem to escape it.

On those days, what do you do with your feelings? Do you try to cover them up so no one will notice? Do you get frustrated with the people around you? Do you talk to anyone? Where can you find help?

The author of today's psalm had a difficult day, too. But rather than hiding his feelings, he decided to share them with God. He decided to be honest— even though it likely felt hard and uncomfortable.

Whatever you are feeling today, you can share it with God. You can tell him what's on your heart and mind. You can even ask him questions. No matter what is happening, or what you say, God is not surprised. He is not upset. He still loves you. He is still trustworthy.

God cares about what's going on in your heart and mind. He invites you to share this with him. He welcomes your honesty, even on the difficult days. He will walk with you no matter what is happening, and no matter what you are feeling. He promises to be with you.

A Closer Look

Make a list of all the troubles the psalmist shares with God. What does he remember about God that helps him in his troubles?

A Closer Look

Write down all the blessings
David mentions in verses 1–5.
Keep reading and write down
how the psalmist describes God
and his love for his children. Are
these things you can also bless
the Lord for? Make this psalm
into your own prayer.

We Are Blessed Because of Jesus
READ PSALM 103

Bless the LORD, O my soul,
    and forget not all his benefits,
who forgives all your iniquity,
    who heals all your diseases,
who redeems your life from the pit,
    who crowns you with steadfast love and mercy. (vv. 2–4)

Have you ever looked ahead in a book? Maybe you were curious about the plot, or maybe you wanted to know the ending. In today's psalm, David looked ahead to a future part of God's story—the day God would take our sins away and forgive us. Today we can look back at that part of God's story knowing God sent his Son Jesus to take the punishment we deserved so we could be forgiven.

David looked ahead and said one day God would remove our sin and put it as far away from us as the east is from the west (verse 12). That means God forgives our sin forever and remembers it no more. Those who turn from their sin to trust in Jesus will never face God's judgment for the bad things we have done.

When David looked ahead in God's story to the work of Jesus, he had only one response: to bless the Lord—to thank him for forgiveness and grace. He repeated the words "Bless the LORD" seven times in this song! Just as Jesus died for the sins of David, he died for your sins too. All the wonderful "benefits" this psalm promises are ours because Jesus died and rose again. Jesus is calling everyone to turn from sin and trust in him. In Jesus, all the blessings of God's children are ours. That's a wonderful reason to bless the Lord!

Hallelujah!
READ PSALMS 104–106

The last three psalms of Book Four end with the Hebrew word *hallelujah*. Hallelujah is made up of two smaller Hebrew words, *halal* and *Yah*. The first word *halal* means "let the people praise" and the second word *Yah* is a short form of the covenant name for God (Yahweh). So the word *hallelujah* means, "let the people praise Yahweh." Most Bibles translate hallelujah in the book of Psalms with the three English words, "praise the Lord."

While most Bible translators didn't use the Hebrew word *hallelujah* in translating the psalms, they do use it in the book of Revelation. Hallelujah shows up four times in Revelation 19, in verses 1, 3, 4, and 6. Here is one of those verses:

"After this I heard what seemed to be the loud voice of a great multitude in heaven, crying out, 'Hallelujah! Salvation and glory and power belong to our God.'" (Revelation 19:1)

The famous music composer Handel repeated the word *Hallelujah* more than fifty times in his famous song, the "Hallelujah Chorus," which is performed at Christmastime all around the world. Handel wanted everyone to "praise the Lord" for sending his Son Jesus to save us from our sin.

The editor of the book of Psalms ends Book Four with three Hallelujah psalms. What a great response after singing that God has removed our sins as far as the east is from the west (Psalm 103). What can you say when singing about God's forgiveness? It seems only one word will do and that is, "Hallelujah!" We've inserted the word *hallelujah* where it belongs in the Psalms.

PSALM 104
Praise the Lord for His Rule over All

"I will sing to the Lord all my life; I will sing praise to my God as long as I live. May my meditation be pleasing to him, as I rejoice in the Lord. But may sinners vanish from the earth and the wicked be no more. Praise the Lord, my soul. Hallelujah." (vv. 33–35 NIV)

Remember the meaning of "hallelujah" (let the people praise the Lord) so that whenever you hear it in a song you remember what it means.

Hallelujah. Give thanks to the LORD, for he is good

Psalm 106:1

PSALM 105
Praise the Lord for His Wondrous Works

"He brought out his people with rejoicing, his chosen ones with shouts of joy; he gave them the lands of the nations, and they fell heir to what others had toiled for——that they might keep his precepts and observe his laws. Hallelujah!" (vv. 43–45 NIV)

The first four verses of Psalm 105 call us to praise by telling others of God's wondrous works. Make a list of the wonderful things God has done in your life, then offer up a prayer of praise to God for all he has done for you.

PSALM 106
Praise the Lord for His Eternal Love

"Hallelujah. Give thanks to the LORD, for he is good; his love endures forever. Who can proclaim the mighty acts of the LORD or fully declare his praise?" (vv. 1–2 NIV)

"Save us, LORD our God, and gather us from the nations, that we may give thanks to your holy name and glory in your praise. Praise be to the LORD, the God of Israel, from everlasting to everlasting. Let all the people say, 'Amen!' Hallelujah." (vv. 47–48 NIV)

Did you know that everything in this life will one day be gone—but God's love will endure forever. For those who trust Jesus, nothing can separate them from God's love (Romans 8:38– 39). Now that's something to shout "Hallelujah!" about!

Chapter Five

Oliver's Story:

God Is Oliver's Refuge and Strength

Oliver's dad, Charles, closed the book. "Well, that's the end of Book Four." He knew Oliver would rather be reading with Grandpa. Charles remembered all the times he had come to the old oak with his father—and how much he cherished it. Oliver was not the only one missing Grandpa. His whole family was sad.

The night before Grandpa went home to Jesus, he called everyone to his bedside to say goodbye. Somehow he knew the end was near. "Promise me two things," Grandpa said, grasping Oliver's hand. "Promise you'll finish the book with your father." Oliver nodded and answered, "I will. I love you, Grandpa."

"One more thing," Grandpa said, looking toward Oliver. "Share what you've learned with others."

Oliver nodded with fresh tears rolling down his cheeks. "I will, Grandpa. 'God is our refuge and strength, an ever-present help in trouble. Therefore we will not fear, though the earth give way and the mountains fall into the heart of the sea.'"

Grandpa smiled and said, "Psalm 46."

Then Oliver said goodnight to his grandfather and hugged him gently. By the morning, Grandpa was in the presence of Jesus.

The weeks following Grandpa's passing were quiet. Mom, Dad, and Oliver spent time sharing memories of Grandpa around the fireplace and on walks through the woods. Their memories seemed to draw them closer together.

Charles and Oliver decided to wait till spring to continue reading the book. And even when spring came, their walk out to the old oak felt strange without Grandpa. But the scene was beautiful—they were surrounded by the blooming crocuses and new buds on the trees. Everything was vibrant and fragrant.

Charles said, "I'm so thankful for spring. You know, Grandpa loved to watch the changing of seasons—especially new life in the spring. Can you imagine all that he's enjoying now in heaven—and that one day we will join him in seeing Jesus face-to-face?"

Just then, Oliver noticed two squirrels racing across the leafy forest floor. They scampered past a little row of green saplings, peeking out of the ground. Oliver looked closer and realized what they were. He shouted, "The saplings! Grandpa told me they'd be here! He reminded me that even though the old oak would one day die, the forest would have new life." He paused. "It reminds me of our new life in Christ—and of the resurrection that's to come. I think spring might be my new favorite season!"

Charles and Oliver spent several hours that afternoon tending to the saplings, enjoying the scents and sights, and marveling at the great wonder of all that was yet to come.

Book

N° 5

Psalms 107–150

LOOKING AHEAD TO HEAVEN WITH PRAISE

Tell Everyone to Come
READ PSALM 107

Let the redeemed of the LORD say so,
    whom he has redeemed from trouble
and gathered in from the lands,
    from the east and from the west,
    from the north and from the south. (vv. 2–3)

Imagine you are on a sports team wins its final championship game. To celebrate, your coach invites everyone to the local ice cream shop across the street from the fields for free ice cream cones. He shouts out at the top of his voice, "Free ice cream for everyone!" That means you, all the players of the team, all your family, friends, and even the umpires are invited to join you. Everyone jumps up and down and shouts, "Hurray!" Then they run and tell everyone in the stands. "We won! Free ice cream for everyone!"

Psalm 107 describes a scene that is a little like winning that championship game, but way better and bigger! Jesus died on the cross to pay the penalty for our sin. He paid the price—that is what redeemed means. Now the way to heaven is open and free for everyone who believes, from every nation. God will gather his children from the east, west, north, and south.

God's free call of grace goes out to people wandering in the desert, people who are in trouble, those who are thirsty and hungry, prisoners, and all people who are living in the darkness of sin. Jesus said, "Come to me, all you who are weary and burdened, and I will give you rest" (Matthew 11:28 NIV).

Did you know God is calling you to come? He is calling each of us by name. Jesus has won the victory for us all and he wants us to join his victory celebration and let everyone know that the way to heaven is free. Jesus paid the price. He has won our victory! Leave your sin and trouble behind and come and believe in Jesus and you can join in the celebration.

The Big Picture
READ PSALM 108

Oh grant us help against the foe,
    for vain is the salvation of man!
With God we shall do valiantly;
    it is he who will tread down our foes. (vv. 12–13)

If you look at an oil painting close up, all you see is a swirl of brush strokes. But when you step back from the painting you see how all the colors and shades work together to create a picture. The different songs in the book of Psalms are like the colors of a painting. But when we step back, just like the painting, the book of Psalms tells a bigger story. The Psalms tells us a story of victory. Just compare Book One with Book Five. There are twice as many laments in Book One than Book Five.

The same is true of our lives. We go through good times and bad, but God wins in the end! Everyone who trusts in Jesus joins the march to victory and sings the praises of Psalm 108:3–4.

"I will give thanks to you, O LORD, among the peoples; I will sing praises to you among the nations. For your steadfast love is great above the heavens; your faithfulness reaches to the clouds." One day God will take all our sadness away and all we will know is joy (Revelation 21:4). Imagine a final victory day when God makes the earth brand-new and God destroys all evil so that nothing bad ever happens again. How can looking forward to that day help us to live for God today?

A Closer Look

Write down all the reasons the psalm writer has for praising God. What does he ask God for? Now try rewriting a few verses as your own psalm of praise for what God has done for you and ask him for victory over the hard things in your life.

A Closer Look

Read Romans 12:17–21 and write down how God wants us to treat our enemies. Remember when someone does something mean or wrong to you, God will be your defender. He stands ready to help. He does see trouble and considers it to take it in hand (Psalm 10:14). Love says no to sin, so if someone is doing bad things to you, you can say, "No!" and ask an adult for help.

God Stands Ready to Help
READ PSALM 109

With my mouth I will give great thanks to the LORD;
    I will praise him in the midst of the throng.
For he stands at the right hand of the needy one,
    to save him from those who condemn his soul to death.
    (vv. 30–31)

When a thief grabs and steals something from a store, the clerk shouts out to a nearby police officer for help! When we see a crime committed, we call 911 for help. When they catch a criminal, they send him to a judge. In Psalm 109 we learn that David faced terrible enemies doing bad things to him. They were even trying to kill him. But David knew God could help. He called out to God in prayer to save him from the people who wanted to kill him.

David asked God to judge his enemies and bring them the same kind of trouble they were bringing to David. When you read David's prayer, are you surprised? Remember these were wicked people doing terrible things to David. But David knew God was a good judge who must punish evil.

The Bible tells us we should not seek revenge against our enemies. Jesus said we should pray for our enemies and do good to them (Matthew 5:44). But you can also pray for God to protect you from anyone who is trying to harm you.

Remember Jesus's example. He knew what it was like to be treated poorly. He even prayed for the soldiers who were crucifying him. If someone is treating you badly, pray for them and be sure to find a trusted adult you can tell and ask for help.

God's Announcement
READ PSALM 110

The LORD says to my Lord:
  "Sit at my right hand,
until I make your enemies your footstool." (v. 1)

When a carnival or show comes to a city, they put up posters to let everyone know about it so they can come. When someone is getting married or having a baby, the person sends announcements through cards or email to tell everyone about the news. But when God wanted to announce that he was sending Jesus, he spoke to the people through prophets to let the people know about his plan. Psalm 110 is a prophecy about God sending his Son Jesus. Look through the psalm and see if you can find a clue that points to Jesus.

Here are some of the clues: We learn that the person God will send sits at God's right hand (v. 1) and that he must be a king because he has a scepter (v. 2). He will rule over his enemies and he will be a priest forever (v. 4). He will also judge the nations (v. 6). Jesus is the only person who fits all of these descriptions.

So, long before Jesus was ever born, King David, inspired by God's Spirit sang this song about Jesus. When the people of Israel heard the words of the song, they knew it was about God's promise to send a king who would live forever and save God's people.

Thank God today for keeping his promise in sending a Rescuer for sinners. Thank him for being in heaven now, praying at the right hand of the Father for you. Thank him that you are fully accepted by God because of Jesus. In Christ, all of God's promises come true! God's announcement to David came true, and it is now yours to enjoy as well!

A Closer Look

What do you think David means when he says in verse 4 that "The Lord has sworn and will not change his mind, 'You are a priest forever after the order of Melchizadek'"? Read Hebrews 7 for the answer.

A Mountain of Hallelujahs
READ PSALMS 111–117

I will give **thanks** to the **LORD** with my *whole* **heart**

After Psalm 110, which so clearly points to Jesus the Messiah, the editor added a pattern of seven psalms that praise the Lord. He placed three "hallelujah psalms" on either side of Psalm 114 which calls us again and again to trust in the salvation of the Lord and lists the many blessings he has given to his people. Psalms 111–113 begin with "Praise the LORD!" which is actually *hallelujah* in Hebrew. Then after we celebrate the salvation of God, in Psalm 114, the next three psalms end with the word *hallelujah*.

Having read about Jesus in Psalm 110, the editor of this wonderful collection is calling us to sing praises to the Lord again and again, leading up to Psalm 118 which also points to Jesus. As you read through these seven psalms, look for the words, "Praise the LORD!" and substitute the word *Hallelujah!* Shout it loud as you read!

Psalm 111
Praise God for
His Works

Psalm 112
Praise God for
His Blessings

Psalm 113
Praise God's Name

"Praise the LORD!
I will give thanks
to the LORD with
my whole heart,
in the company of
the upright, in the
congregation. Great
are the works of the
LORD, studied by all
who delight in them.
Full of splendor
and majesty is
his work, and his
righteousness
endures forever."
(vv. 1–3)

God calls us to love
him with all our heart,
soul, and strength
(Deuteronomy 6:5).
That is how the
writer of Psalm 111
begins his song of
praise. What would
it look like for you
to love God with all
your heart, soul, and
strength today?

"Praise the LORD!
Blessed is the
man who fears the
LORD, who greatly
delights in his
commandments!
His offspring will be
mighty in the land;
the generation of
the upright will be
blessed." (vv. 1–2)

Psalm 112 lists the
benefits that come to
a person who trusts in
the Lord. How many
benefits from trusting
God can you find in
this psalm? Which one
most encourages you
to trust in the Lord?

"Praise the LORD!
Praise, O servants
of the LORD, praise
the name of the
LORD! Blessed be the
name of the LORD
from this time forth
and forevermore!
From the rising
of the sun to its
setting, the name
of the LORD is to be
praised!"
(vv. 1–3)

This psalm goes on to
say God rules above
all looking down
upon the earth, ready
to help those in need
who call upon him.
Take some time to
consider God in his
majesty sitting on
his throne above all
the earth. Offer your
prayers to him and ask
him to help you live
for him.

Psalm 114
Praise God for Our Salvation

"Tremble, O earth, at the presence of the Lord, at the presence of the God of Jacob, who turns the rock into a pool of water, the flint into a spring of water." (vv. 7–8)

Remembering God's great deeds gives us reason and fresh motivation to praise him. Look up one of the events the psalmist mentions, like Israel's rescue from Egypt (Exodus 1–13), the opening of the Red Sea (Exodus 14), or the crossing of the Jordan (Joshua 3).

Psalm 115
Praise God Forever

"The heavens are the LORD's heavens, but the earth he has given to the children of man. The dead do not praise the LORD, nor do any who go down into silence. But we will bless the LORD from this time forth and forevermore. Praise the LORD!" (vv. 16–18)

People all over the world still worship gods carved from stone and wood. Read through the comparison between our living God and a dead idol. What in this psalm encourages you to live for our living God?

Psalm 116
Praise God for He Hears Our Prayers

"I will offer to you the sacrifice of thanksgiving and call on the name of the LORD. I will pay my vows to the LORD in the presence of all his people, in the courts of the house of the LORD, in your midst, O Jerusalem. Praise the LORD!" (vv. 17–19)

Psalm 116 is a song written about an answered prayer. How can reading this testimony help build our faith to trust God to hear and answer our prayers? What prayers of yours has God said, "Yes" to?

Psalm 117
Praise God for His Steadfast Love

"Praise the LORD, all nations! Extol him, all peoples! For great is his steadfast love toward us, and the faithfulness of the LORD endures forever. Praise the LORD!" (vv. 1–2)

Psalm 117 is the shortest psalm in the Bible. Take time today to memorize this psalm. Take a peek ahead at Psalm 118. Why do you think the editor put this psalm just ahead of Psalm 118?

Ezra 3:11

Give Thanks
READ PSALM 118

Oh give thanks to the LORD, for he is good;
    for his steadfast love endures forever! (v. 1)

As soon as the last stone of the new temple foundation was put into place, the trumpets blared and the cymbals crashed. The people of Israel gave thanks to the Lord and sang the words of Psalm 118, "He is good, for his steadfast love endures forever" (Ezra 3:11). They repeated these words of thanksgiving from Psalm 118 again and again.

Words from this psalm were also shouted when Jesus came riding into Jerusalem on a donkey, the week before he died. The Sunday before his death, as Jesus road into Jerusalem the people laid their cloaks on the ground in front of him, waved palm branches at him, and shouted verse 26 of Psalm 118, "Hosanna! Blessed is he who comes in the name of the Lord, even the King of Israel!" (John 12:13).

Take a moment to think of all the reasons why you are thankful for what God has done for you. Is he good? Does he walk with you through difficult times? Take a moment to create a list of praises. Be sure to thank God for the greatest praise of all: sending his only Son, Jesus, to be your Savior. Rejoice in his great rescue for you on the cross and the great hope of eternal life.

Today when you gather for a meal, take a moment and have everyone share one thing God has done for them. Then after each one, repeat the words of Psalm 118. Or ask family or friends to gather together to share praises to God. You can share words, prayers, or songs. As you each take turns sharing, listen well to each other and then respond with the words: *Oh give thanks to the LORD, for he is good; his steadfast love endures forever!*

A Closer Look

Read through Psalm 118 and count how many times the psalm repeat the words, "His steadfast love endures forever." Write down some ways you have seen God's steadfast love to you this past year. Then thank God for his steadfast love.

Do You Know Your ABCs?
READ PSALM 119

Your word is a lamp to my feet
and a light to my path. (v. 105)

Psalm 119 follows the Hebrew alphabet. Each section of the psalm begins with a different letter and every line in that section also begins with that same letter. In English the first line of each section might look something like this:

Arise and worship before the Lord
Bless the Lord with singing
Call out to him with all your voice
Declare his praise before the world
Exalt the Lord and tell of his mighty works
For the Lord is good and his mercy endures forever.

Do you see how the pattern works? We call a poem or song that follows this kind of pattern an acrostic. The first Hebrew letter is *Aleph*, the second is *Beth*. It looks like it was written to help people memorize all the ways God's Word helps us. From *Aleph* to *Taw*, or as we would say, from *A* to *Z*.

Psalm 119 is an acrostic poem that helps us to remember all the blessings that come from reading and thinking about God's Word. This is the longest psalm in the Bible. But don't get overwhelmed! Try reading Psalm 119 in sections. Take one section each day and ask yourself the following questions: What is God teaching me about his Word? What blessings will I receive from obeying God's Word?

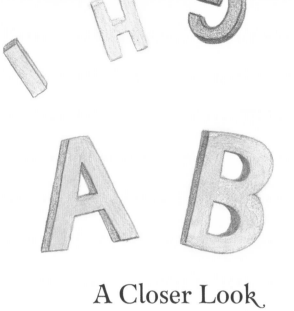

A Closer Look

As you read look for other things the psalm writer talks about.
Circle any part where he confesses his sins. Draw a square
around any words that describe God and what he has
done for him. Then underline all the phrases that
list the blessings of God's Word.

A Song for Each Step
READ PSALMS 120–126

There is a story behind the next group of psalms. Each of these psalms is labeled "A Psalm of Ascents." Psalms 120–126 and the eight psalms that follow form their own short songbook. Bible teachers believe these fifteen songs were sung as the people of Israel ascended (which means climbed) the fifteen steps that led up to the temple court. It could be that the people of Israel sang these short songs one at a time as they climbed each of the stairs.

There are seven psalms of ascent before Psalm 127 and seven more after. Two of the first seven were written by King David during the days of the first temple. Two of the last seven were also written by David. Bible teachers believe the five before and the five after with no name listed were written during the time of the second temple.

As you read through the Psalms written by King David, think of the first temple (1 Kings 6) and how amazing it was to walk the steps up to a temple where you knew God lived. When you read the other psalms of ascent, written during the time of second temple, imagine you are a young Israelite walking the fifteen steps up to a newly rebuilt temple after living as a captive in Babylon. Think of how excited you would be to praise God for bringing you back to your land and for helping you rebuild your city. As you read each of these psalms, try to imagine what the writers were thinking about as they climbed the steps. Use their ideas to form your own prayer to God.

PSALM 120 (A Song of Ascents)
Call on God in Times of Trouble

"In my distress I called to the LORD, and he answered me." (v. 1)

God loves to deliver us from our troubles. Do you have any troubles you could call upon God and ask him to deliver you from?

PSALM 121 (A Song of Ascents)
Remember My Help Comes from the LORD

"I lift up my eyes to the hills. From where does my help come?
My help comes from the LORD, who made heaven and earth."
(vv. 1–2)

While we get tired and must sleep to stay
healthy, God never gets tired, and he never
sleeps. God is always watching over you.
Make Psalm 121 your prayer to God and ask
him to be your help and protection.

PSALM 122
(A Song of Ascents of David)
Give Thanks to God

"I was glad when they said to me, 'Let us go to the house of the LORD!' Our feet have been standing within your gates, O Jerusalem! Jerusalem—built as a city that is bound firmly together, to which the tribes go up, the tribes of the LORD, as was decreed for Israel, to give thanks to the name of the LORD." (vv. 1–4)

David said he was glad when he was asked to go up to the house of the Lord. How do you feel about going to church on Sunday to worship God? When your mom and dad call out, "It's time for church," are you glad to go worship God?

PSALM 123
(A Song of Ascents)
Pray for God's Mercy

"To you I lift up my eyes, O you who are enthroned in the heavens! Behold, as the eyes of servants look to the hand of their master, as the eyes of a maidservant to the hand of her mistress, so our eyes look to the LORD our God, till he has mercy upon us." (vv. 1–2)

God doesn't always immediately answer our prayers. Often he calls us to wait patiently. The psalmist writes, "Our eyes look to the LORD our God, till he has mercy on us." Do you have a prayer God hasn't yet answered? If so, pray it again and wait for God to answer you.

PSALM 124
(A Song of Ascents of David)
Remember God Is Our Defender

"If it had not been the LORD who was on our side—let Israel now say—if it had not been the LORD who was on our side when people rose up against us, then they would have swallowed us up alive, when their anger was kindled against us; then the flood would have swept us away, the torrent would have gone over us; then over us would have gone the raging waters." (vv. 1–5)

One of the best things we can do before we go to church on Sunday is remember all that God has done for us in the past. Try thinking about all the ways God has protected you next Sunday morning and go to church full of thanksgiving for God's help.

PSALM 125
(A Song of Ascents)
Remember God Is
Our Protector

"Those who trust in the Lord are like Mount Zion, which cannot be moved, but abides forever. As the mountains surround Jerusalem, so the Lord surrounds his people, from this time forth and forevermore." (vv. 1–2)

Notice that the strength of the people described as an immovable mountain (v. 1) comes from the presence of God and his power (v. 2). Which of the two groups described in the psalm are you a part of, those who trust the Lord or those who turn aside?

PSALM 126
(A Song of Ascents)
Rejoice and Be Glad

"When the Lord restores the fortunes of Zion, we were like those who dream. Then our mouth was filled with laughter, and our tongue with shouts of joy; then they said among the nations, 'The Lord has done great things for them.' The Lord has done great things for us; we are glad." (vv. 1–3)

Imagine how excited the people of Judah, who were living as captives for seventy years far from home, were to return home to Jerusalem. Where is God asking you to trust him and be patient to wait for him to deliver you from your trouble? Allow this psalm to strengthen your faith.

A Closer Look

Where do you need God's help today? Where will you need it tomorrow? Share your heart with him now. He will be faithful. Write out a prayer asking God to help you with something you are trying to do. Be sure to also write down how God answered that prayer and remember to thank him.

We Need God's Help
READ PSALM 127

Unless the LORD builds the house,
    those who build it labor in vain.
Unless the LORD watches over the city,
    the watchman stays awake in vain. (v. 1)

Have you ever asked an adult to help you build a fort or playhouse? Kids love to build things, but it is really hard to build something all by yourself. Once an adult joins in to help, the fort is finished in no time!

Psalm 127 reminds us that we can't do life on our own. We need God's help. God is glad to help us and only wants us to ask him. God is ready to help us in school, at home, and when we play. God helps dads and moms build their families, and God is at work helping pastors build the church. If we try to do things without God, Solomon tells us we will "labor in vain." That means things will not work out for us. When we try to do things without God, you can be sure that he will teach us how much we need him.

Can you think of a time when you asked for God's help, and he answered? Did he provide peace when you were angry? Did he give you peace when you were worried? Did he comfort you when you were sad? Think of all the ways he has helped you, and be sure to thank him.

The Last Seven Steps
READ PSALMS 128–134

King Solomon built the first temple in Jerusalem around 950 years before Jesus was born. It took seven years to complete. When the work was finished, the cloud of God's glory came down from heaven and filled the temple in the sight of all the people (1 Kings 8:11). From then on, the people traveled three times a year to worship at the temple (Deuteronomy 16:16), for God lived there among his people.

350 years later, as generations past, the people of Israel turned away from God to worship idols. So, God sent King Nebuchadnezzar to break down the walls of Jerusalem and destroy the temple (Jeremiah 52). Nebuchadnezzar's army captured the Israelites and took them back to Babylon where they lived in exile, away from their homes, for seventy years. Then God raised up men like Nehemiah and Zerubbabel to return to Jerusalem to rebuild the walls of the city and restore the temple.

Imagine what it would be like for a young boy or girl to return home and see the men building a new temple. While Psalms 128–134 were written during the time of the first temple, it was during the days of the restored temple that the people of Israel sang these fifteen psalms of ascent as they climbed up the stairs to the temple above. Even though the temple was destroyed again after Jesus died, the fifteen steps are still there today. If you go to Jerusalem, you can still climb them and sing these songs of prayer and praise to God.

PSALM 128 (A Song of Ascents)
Blessed Are Those Who Fear the Lord

"Blessed is everyone who fears the Lord, who walks in his ways! You shall eat the fruit of the labor of your hands; you shall be blessed, and it shall be well with you." (vv. 1–2)

Fearing God means honoring him and loving him before everything else. When you love God, you want to do what he loves. That's what we call obedience. Jesus is the only human to ever have feared God with all his heart, soul, and mind. That's good news for us when we fail. Because Jesus died for our sins, we can trust in his perfect record. Review this psalm and make a list of the benefits that come from fearing the Lord.

Blessed
is everyone who
fears the LORD,
who walks in his ways!

Psalm 128:1

PSALM 129 (A Song of Ascents)
The Lord Is Our Righteous Defender

"The LORD is righteous; he has cut the cords of the wicked." (v. 4)

It is a good thing to share our troubles honestly when we pray to God. Using Psalm 129 as an example, share your challenges and troubles with God in prayer. Then declare your trust in God to deliver you.

PSALM 130 (A Song of Ascents)
Put Your Hope in God

"O Israel, hope in the LORD! For with the Lord there is steadfast love, and with him is plentiful redemption." (v. 7)

Satan tries to condemn us for our sins so we turn away from God. But again, and again we see the psalm writers confess their sin to God and then remind themselves that God is merciful and forgiving. Turn to God and confess your sin and ask for his forgiveness.

PSALM 131 (A Song of Ascents of David)
Hope in the Lord Forevermore

"O Israel, hope in the Lord from this time forth and forevermore." (v. 3)

Our hope is found in God alone. The psalmist tells us our hope is in God forevermore! When you wake up tomorrow morning, ask God to help you put all of your hope in him.

PSALM 132 (A Song of Ascents)
God Keeps His Promises

"For the sake of your servant David, do not turn away the face of your anointed one. The Lord swore to David a sure oath from which he will not turn back: 'One of the sons of your body I will set on your throne. If your sons keep my covenant and my testimonies that I shall teach them, their sons also forever shall sit on your throne.'" (vv. 10–12)

Read through this psalm and notice how Jesus fulfills the promises in this psalm. Then praise God for his salvation through Jesus using the words of this psalm.

PSALM 133 (A Song of Ascents of David)
Pray for Unity

"Behold, how good and pleasant it is when brothers dwell in unity! It is like the precious oil on the head, running down on the beard, on the beard of Aaron, running down on the collar of his robes! It is like the dew of Hermon, which falls on the mountains of Zion! For there the Lord has commanded the blessing, life forevermore." (vv. 1–3)

Unity is so important to God that he tells us to make it more important than our worship (see Matthew 5:23–24). Do you have a strained or broken relationship within someone else? If so, look for an opportunity to be reconciled with your brother or sister.

PSALM 134 (A Song of Ascents)
Bless the Lord and Praise Him

"Come, bless the Lord, all you servants of the Lord, who stand by night in the house of the Lord! Lift up your hands to the holy place and bless the Lord! May the Lord bless you from Zion, he who made heaven and earth!" (vv. 1–3)

This last psalm of ascent calls those who served guard at the temple through the watches of the night to "bless the Lord." So too should we bless the Lord at all times. We praise him on Sunday, but also when we work and when we play. Anytime is a good time to praise the Lord!

For with
the
LORD
there is
steadfast
love,

and with him is plentiful redemption.

Psalm 130:7

Remember and Hope in the Lord

READ PSALMS 135–137

The psalms teach us how to fight against worry, fear, and doubt. Start by remembering how God has helped you in the past and then remind yourself of God's great presence, power, and steadfast love today and place your hope in him. That is how the psalm writers encouraged Israel. The people of Israel made it through tough times by singing songs that retold the history of how God saved his people. Here, right in the middle of the last book of Psalms, the editor gives us three historical psalms that celebrate what God has done and remind us of his greatness.

Sing Psalm 135 to remember how powerful God is. God controls the lightning and wind. God is more powerful than kings and nations. Next, remember that God's love is steadfast—that means it is strong and can't be moved and his love lasts forever. Psalm 136 repeats this twenty-six times! Psalm 137 remembers the terrible days when the people of Israel were captive in Babylon and calls out to God to judge their enemies.

Psalm 135
Remember God Is All-Powerful

"For I know that the LORD is great, and that our LORD is above all gods. Whatever the LORD pleases, he does, in heaven and on earth, in the seas and all deeps. He it is who makes the clouds rise at the end of the earth, who makes lightnings for the rain and brings forth the wind from his storehouses." (vv. 5–7)

Remembering the mighty deeds of the Lord helps to build our faith to trust God through our present trials. How does this psalm help you to trust God for the challenges you face?

Psalm 136
Remember God's Love Lasts Forever

"To him who spread out the earth above the waters, for his steadfast love endures forever; to him who made the great lights, for his steadfast love endures forever; the sun to rule over the day, for his steadfast love endures forever; the moon and stars to rule over the night, for his steadfast love endures forever; to him who struck down the firstborn of Egypt, for his steadfast love endures forever; and brought Israel out from among them, for his steadfast love endures forever; with a strong hand and an outstretched arm, for his steadfast love endures forever; to him who divided the Red Sea in two, for his steadfast love endures forever." (vv. 6–13)

Memorize the refrain, "His steadfast love endures forever." Make a list of five things God has done for you and after you write each one recite the refrain as your prayer of thanks and praise to God.

Psalm 137
Never Forget God

"If I forget you, O Jerusalem, let my right hand forget its skill! Let my tongue stick to the roof of my mouth, if I do not remember you, if I do not set Jerusalem above my highest joy!" (vv. 5–6)

The musicians of God's temple, never forgot the songs they sang at the temple in Jerusalem through all the seventy years of captivity in Babylon (see Ezra 3:10). No matter what trial you go through, take the Psalms with you. Pray that God will help you to never forget to praise him.

Where shall I go from your Spirit?

Or where shall I flee from your presence?

Psalm 139:7

The Last Psalms of King David
READ PSALMS 138–144

Psalms 138–145 form the final collection of King David's songs. Few men trusted God through difficulty more than King David. His songs remind us that God answers our prayers (Psalm 138:3), God is always with us (Psalm 139:7), God protects us in the day of battle (Psalm 140:7), God can keep us from evil (Psalm 141:4), God is our refuge (Psalms 142:5; 144:1–2), and God preserves our life in times of trouble (Psalm 143:11). While the book of Psalms ends with joy-filled celebration, these last laments remind us that we will have trials in life until the very end when Jesus returns.

God gave us the Psalms to help us in our struggles. Which one of these psalms is a helpful prayer for you?

PSALM 138
God Answers Our Prayers

"I give you thanks, O Lord, with my whole heart; before the gods I sing your praise; I bow down toward your holy temple and give thanks to your name for your steadfast love and your faithfulness, for you have exalted above all things your name and your word. On the day I called, you answered me; my strength of soul you increased." (vv. 1–3)

Even when David's troubles didn't go away, he believed God walked with him (v. 7). What most comforts you in this psalm? How can you use it during a hard time as your prayer to God, trusting he will help and deliver you?

PSALM 139
God Is Always with Us

"Where shall I go from your Spirit? Or where shall I flee from your presence? If I ascend to heaven, you are there! If I make my bed in Sheol, you are there! If I take the wings of the morning and dwell in the uttermost parts of the sea, even there your hand shall lead me, and your right hand shall hold me." (vv. 7–10)

God knows all our thoughts and watches over all our ways. None of us can hide or run away from God. Wherever you go, God will be there too. This truth is both a comfort and a warning. Is there anything in your life you are trying to hide from God? Confess your hidden sin and run to him.

PSALM 140
God Protects Us in the
Day of Battle

"I say to the Lord, You are my
God; give ear to the voice of
my pleas for mercy, O Lord!
O Lord, my Lord, the strength
of my salvation, you have
covered my head in the day
of battle. Grant not, O Lord,
the desires of the wicked; do
not further their evil plot, or
they will be exalted!"
(vv. 6—8)

While you may not
have violent men
hunting for you, we all
face fearful challenges
from time to time. What
fears do you struggle
with? Take some time
and use Psalm 140 to
guide your prayer for
help to trust the Lord in
the midst of your fears.

PSALM 141
God Can Keep Us from Evil

"Set a guard, O Lord, over my
mouth; keep watch over the
door of my lips! Do not let
my heart incline to any evil,
to busy myself with wicked
deeds in company with men
who work iniquity, and let me
not eat of their delicacies!"
(vv. 3—4)

As a part of the Lord's
prayer, Jesus said we
should ask God to "lead
us not into temptation."
That is the theme of
Psalm 141. Using this
psalm as a guide, ask
God to help you say no
to sin and temptation
and ask him to help
you live for him.

PSALM 142
God Is Our Refuge

"I cry to you, O Lord; I say,
'You are my refuge, my
portion in the land of the
living.' Attend to my cry, for I
am brought very low! Deliver
me from my persecutors, for
they are too strong for me!"
(vv. 5—6)

When David is
struggling, he knows
he can run to God.
He is not afraid to
offer up a complaint
to God (v. 2), but he
does so respectfully,
declaring his trust in
God (v. 5). That is a
pattern you can follow
in your prayers.

PSALM 143
God Protects Our Life in Times of Trouble

"For your name's sake, O Lord, preserve my life! In your righteousness bring my soul out of trouble! And in your steadfast love you will cut off my enemies, and you will destroy all the adversaries of my soul, for I am your servant."
(vv. 11–12)

Add the following phrases to your prayer this morning. Start with "Hear my prayer, O Lord" (v. 1) and end with "answer me quickly, O Lord" (v. 7). What a comfort to know God wants us to pray this way. Why else would he give us these psalms?

PSALM 144
God Is My Help and My Strength

"Blessed be the Lord, my rock, who trains my hands for war, and my fingers for battle; he is my steadfast love and my fortress, my stronghold and my deliverer, my shield and he in whom I take refuge, who subdues peoples under me." (vv. 1–2)

Psalm 18 is similar to this one. Compare the two to find out where they are the same and where they are different. We can turn to the Lord again and again with the same prayers we prayed yesterday and not be concerned that he will turn us away.

From Generation to Generation
READ PSALM 145

**One generation shall commend your works to another,
and shall declare your mighty acts. (v. 4)**

Everyone is old enough to tell others about God. Even children can tell other kids about God. Do you have a younger brother or sister? If you do, you can tell them about the good things God does, just like your parents tell you. Telling others is the way God planned for his Word to spread.

That is what David announces in Psalm 145. He tells us that "one generation shall commend your works to another, and shall declare your mighty acts." Then the whole psalm is a list of the ways David has seen God bless his people. David tells us God does mighty acts, "wondrous works, and awesome deeds" (vv. 4–6). David tells us God is gracious and merciful, slow to anger and abounding in steadfast love" (v. 8). David knew the words he wrote would help his children and grandchildren learn about God.

A Closer Look

What about you? What has God done for you? Who can you tell what God has done for you? If you can't think of something, tell someone about God from the Bible stories you know. Tell others about Jesus and all he has done.

We Have More Reason to Praise
READ PSALMS 146–149

The editor who put the book of Psalms together ended the collection with five more hallelujah psalms. These last five praise songs all begin and end with the Hebrew word *hallelujah* ("Praise the LORD" in English). As we read these wonderful songs, let us remember that we have more reason to praise. Back when these songs were first composed, the people were waiting for their salvation to come. Jesus wasn't born yet. The people could only hope for a day when God saved his people. Our voices should be louder because we sing knowing we are saved. Jesus has come!

Psalm 146 begins with this call: "Do not put your trust in princes, in human beings, who cannot save" (v. 3 NIV). If you can't put your trust in a human king, how can God's promise to David for an eternal throne ever be fulfilled? The answer of course is found in Jesus. Jesus is the promised son of David (Psalm 132:10–12) who took up the throne and now reigns forever (Psalm 146:10).

Jesus is the only Prince who can save us. So, as we read through these last five psalms, we should shout louder than any Israelite of old. So raise your voice and shout, "Hallelujah, Praise the LORD!"

PSALM 146
Praise the Lord Who Remains Faithful Forever

"Praise the LORD! Praise the LORD, my soul! I will praise the LORD all my life; I will sing praise to my God as long as I live. Do not put your trust in princes, in human beings, who cannot save. When their spirit departs, they return to the ground; on that very day their plans come to nothing. Blessed are those whose help is the God of Jacob, whose hope is in the LORD their God. He is the Maker of heaven and earth, the sea, and everything in them—he remains faithful forever." (vv. 1–6 NIV)

Which reason to praise listed in this psalm is the best reason to praise God? Which one makes you want to praise the Lord? Take time to offer a prayer of praise to God in your own words.

Praise the LORD!

PSALM 147
Praise the Lord Who Heals the Brokenhearted

"Praise the Lord. How good it is to sing praises to our God, how pleasant and fitting to praise him! The Lord builds up Jerusalem; he gathers the exiles of Israel. He heals the brokenhearted and binds up their wounds." (vv. 1–3 NIV)

Imagine trying to name the few hundred stars you can see in the night sky. God knows each of the trillions of trillions of stars by name. Praise God for his wonderful creation and his awesome power to create all that we see around us.

PSALM 148
Let Everyone and Everything Praise the Lord

"Praise the Lord from the earth, you great sea creatures and all ocean depths, lightning and hail, snow and clouds, stormy winds that do his bidding, you mountains and all hills, fruit trees and all cedars, wild animals and all cattle, small creatures and flying birds, kings of the earth and all nations, you princes and all rulers on earth, young men and women, old men and children. Let them praise the name of the Lord, for his name alone is exalted; his splendor is above the earth and the heavens. And he has raised up for his people a horn, the praise of all his faithful servants, of Israel, the people close to his heart. Praise the Lord." (vv. 7–14 NIV) (The horn is a symbol of a powerful son of David God promised to raise up and is first mentioned in Psalm 132:17)

Zechariah, the father of John the Baptist, prophesied that God would raise up a horn of salvation and his son John would prepare the way for him (Luke 1:68–69). How does knowing that help us understand verse 14 of this psalm?

PSALM 149
Praise the Lord Who Saves Us

"Praise the Lord! Sing to the Lord a new song, his praise in the assembly of the godly! Let Israel be glad in his Maker; let the children of Zion rejoice in their King! Let them praise his name with dancing, making melody to him with tambourine and lyre! For the Lord takes pleasure in his people; he adorns the humble with salvation." (vv. 1–4)

Once again the psalmist calls us to "sing to the Lord a new song." Just as the psalm writers did, we can put our prayers to music. God doesn't care if our songs rhyme and he doesn't judge our voices or our melody. Try singing your prayers to God or making up your own praise song to thank him.

Praise the LORD, my soul!
I will praise the LORD all my life;

Psalm 146:1

Party Time!
READ PSALM 150

Let everything that has breath praise the Lord!
Praise the Lord! (v. 6)

Psalm 150 is one big God party. There is only one way to end such a wonderful book. We need to dance and sing praises to God. We need to praise God with trumpets, guitars, violins, and loud crashing symbols. Once you learn about how wonderful God is, you can't hold it in. You have to shout his praise and celebrate! Everyone is invited to the party. "Let everything that has breath praise the Lord."

The best reason for praising God is that he sent his Son Jesus to die on the cross for our sins so we could be forgiven. Jesus is the one who lived the perfect life of Psalm 1 and the one who died in our place in Psalm 22. We learned he is an eternal King in Psalm 45 and a priest forever in Psalm 110.

We learned we can't do life by ourselves in Psalm 127. In Psalm 23 we learned God is our Good Shepherd who is always with us and always ready to help us. After learning all of that (and more!), it is time to celebrate and praise.

Allow praise to fill your every breath—to enter every thought, word, and conversation. Take the prayers and praise of the Psalms with you wherever you go. Let them guide your own prayers and praise. Let everything within you praise the Lord!

Oliver's Story:

A Gift for Others

Back at the farmhouse, Oliver closed the book called *WonderFull*. He wrote a short note on a piece of paper and folded it over the cover. It read, "A gift for others." Then he set the book back on the shelf.

Oliver looked out the window. He saw the crimson tree line that went on for miles. He saw the sugar maples and the old oak. Oliver loved this farm! He loved all of the memories and all God had done in their midst. He longed to continue Grandpa's legacy. He prayed from Psalm 96:3, "Help me tell the nations about your glory. Help me tell all people about the wonderful things you have done." One day, he planned to read Grandpa's favorite book to his son, under the same old oak tree.

Going Deeper

A WONDERFULL STUDY OF TWENTY-FIVE PSALMS

There is so much to study in the book of Psalms. We thought you might like to learn a bit more about a few of them. The following study dives a bit deeper into five psalms from each of the five sub-books of the Psalms. For each of these twenty-five Psalms we've provided a key teaching point for you to remember and apply to other Psalms. We've also provided you with a question. Read the questions, then read the psalm and see if you can answer it yourself, before reading the listed answer which follows. Hopefully, you will continue reading, studying, and memorizing the Psalms to mine their treasures for the rest of your life.

Psalm 1

KEY IDEA:

The introduction to a book is always important.

QUESTION TO ANSWER:

How does Psalm 1 set the stage for the rest of the book?

God is the center of all the psalms. Psalm 1 is an invitation to delight in God and live for him. It is an appeal to turn from the sins of the world and study God's Word. The rest of the psalms that follow help us fulfill this call. But we have a problem: none of us is able to follow the call of the first two verses of Psalm 1. We are all sinners who turn away from God's way and go our own way. We hurt others. We hurt ourselves. We are not like a tree planted by the stream. We are like a tree withering in drought.

So who can save us? The good news is that Jesus fulfilled the call of Psalm 1. He delighted in God's law and obeyed it completely. Even though we fail to measure up, everyone who trusts in Jesus receives his perfect record and the blessings that come to him. That is how we can become the trees by the stream. Even though we make mistakes and sin, God's judgment will never blow us away like the chaff. Why? Because Jesus takes away our sin and gives us his perfect obedience. When you believe in Jesus and trust in his death on the cross to take away your sin, he sends his Holy Spirit to live inside of you and help you to love, obey, and live like the tree by the stream and bear good fruit. God also promises to write his law upon the hearts of all those who turn to Jesus and believe (Jeremiah 31:33). What a great way to start this wonderful book.

Psalm 2

Look for New Testament connections when you read the Psalms.

How does the story of King Herod sound a lot like the first three verses of Psalm 2?

Nine hundred years before the birth of Christ, the Holy Spirit spoke through King David to write this psalm (Acts 4:25). Peter quoted verse 7 and said it was a prophecy about Jesus and his resurrection (Acts 13:33). Looking back we can also see how verses 2–4 point forward to Jesus. Not long after Jesus was born, the wise men brought news of his birth to King Herod. He asked the wise men to send word back to him once they found the child. But the wise men did not do as Herod wanted. "Then Herod, when he saw that he had been tricked by the wise men, became furious, and he sent and killed all the male children in Bethlehem and in all that region who were two years old or under, according to the time that he had ascertained from the wise men" (Matthew 2:16). God the Father protected his Son, warning Joseph to take him safely away to Egypt until Herod died (Matthew 2:19).

When it was time for his ministry to begin, on the day of his baptism, God the Father fulfilled the prophesied decree of verse 7 saying, "This is my beloved Son, with whom I am well pleased" (Matthew 3:17).

Psalm 14

KEY IDEA:

Pay attention to the ways New Testament authors applied the Psalms.

QUESTION TO ANSWER:

How does Paul use this psalm in Romans 3:9–12?

The writers of the New Testament often quoted passages from Psalms and used them to help explain the gospel. In the book of Romans, the apostle Paul wanted to help the Jews in Rome understand they were sinners, just like the Gentiles (everyone who wasn't a Jew). Paul wanted to be sure the Jews understood they were sinners too, who needed Jesus to save them from their sin. Some of the Jews would be tempted to think they were better than the Gentiles. Paul makes it clear that no one is good or can be good apart from Jesus. We are all sinners who need a Savior.

By quoting from Psalm 14, he was using a Scripture they knew to argue his point. That would help them accept his message. So what about us? Are we all sinners too? Psalm 14 and Romans 3 are clear—not a single one of us has done good. We are all sinners who need to be saved from the punishment we deserve for our rebellion against God.

But, just as the editor of the Psalms included Psalm 16 to provide the good news, so the apostle Paul goes on to explain the good news in Romans 3:21–26. Our righteousness comes from believing in Jesus Christ. It is our faith, not our works that save us. So just as David said, we must take refuge in Jesus for we have no good apart from him (Psalm 16:1–2).

Psalm 22

Look for connections in the Psalms to the cross.

What are the ways Psalm 22 is a prophecy that tells us about Jesus's death on the cross?

Even though Psalm 22 was written a thousand years before Jesus was born, it describes Jesus's crucifixion so well that you might think it was written after his death. The Bible tells us the details of the cross took place according to God's plan (Acts 2:23). Compare verse 18 with John's gospel:

"When the soldiers had crucified Jesus, they took his garments and divided them into four parts, one part for each soldier; also his tunic. But the tunic was seamless, woven in one piece from top to bottom, so they said to one another, 'Let us not tear it, but cast lots for it to see whose it shall be.' This was to fulfill the Scripture which says, 'They divided my garments among them, and for my clothing they cast lots.'" (John 19:23–24)

Here are other verses that directly describe Jesus's death on the cross:

"All who see me mock me." Psalm 22:7; Matthew 27:30–31, 41

"They wag their heads." Psalm 22:7; Matthew 27:39

""He trusts in the Lord; let him deliver him." Psalm 22:8; Matthew 27:43

"My tongue sticks to my jaws." Psalm 22:15; John 19:28

"A company of evildoers encircles me." Psalm 22:16 & Matthew 27:41

"They have pierced my hands and feet." Psalm 22:16 & John 19:18 & 20:25

The beatings Jesus endured dried up his strength like a broken piece of clay pot (Psalm 22:15) and he lost so much water you could count his ribs (Psalm 22:17). The religious rulers opened their mouths wide (Psalm 22:13) to mock Jesus as they gloated and stared, finding their pleasure in his suffering (Psalm 22:17).

While the soldiers caused Jesus terrible suffering, the most painful part of the cross for Jesus was when God his Father turned his face away from helping his only Son and instead judged him guilty for our sin. Jesus, who never sinned, took upon himself the sin of all those who God called to be his sons and daughters; all of us who would one day place our trust in Jesus. God the Father punished Jesus in our place.

While David wrote Psalm 22 about the trials of his own life, when we read Psalm 22 we see in it the story of the cross.

Psalm 32

KEY IDEA:

Learn to identify a penitential psalm.

QUESTION TO ANSWER:

What is a penitential psalm?

Psalm 32 is a penitential psalm. The word *penitential* means to express regret or sadness for your sins (the breaking of God's commands). A penitential psalm shares the author's sorrow for his sin. These psalms often include a confession and a promise to change or turn away from sin. There are seven penitential psalms: 6, 32, 38, 51, 102, 130, and 143.

In this psalm David tells us that when he hid his sin ("kept silent" in v. 3) he couldn't stop thinking about what he did and it bothered him all day and night (v. 4). He said it made him feel terrible inside, like his bones were wasting away (v. 3). But when David confessed his sin and brought it out into the open, God forgave him and his struggle turned to blessing (vv. 1–2). We can't make our sin go away by lying or pretending it is not there. But God can cover our sin with his forgiveness if we bring it out into the open and confess and ask God to forgive us. How about you? How do you feel when you try to hide your sin? Trying to hide it never makes it go away. Only forgiveness can take away our sin.

David warns us to listen to what he says and not be like a horse and mule who lack sense. Those animals have to be tied with ropes because they don't know the right thing to do. We need to listen carefully and ask the Holy Spirit to help us put what David said into practice. We should confess our sins and bring them out into the light so we can be forgiven. Once we give our lives to Jesus, we don't have to fear judgment for Jesus's sacrifice covers our sin. We know when we confess our sin he forgives us (1 John 1:9). Let's follow David's advice who said, "Let everyone who is godly offer prayer to you at a time when you may be found" (v. 6), and confess our sins to God in our prayers. Then thank him for the forgiveness he freely offers us in Jesus.

Psalm 42

KEY IDEA:

Don't skip over things you don't understand. Study them instead.

QUESTION TO ANSWER:

Who was Korah and who were his sons?

While a lot of folks have heard of King David and his son Solomon, not many people are familiar with the sons of Korah, yet they wrote more than ten of the Psalms. Psalms 42, 44–49, 85, and 87–88.

You can read Korah's story in Numbers 16. Korah was given the honor of carrying the ark of God. The ark was the very place where God's presence lived. But Korah complained. Korah rebelled against God and Moses, and he and his family were swallowed up into the earth and destroyed. But later in the Bible we learn that the sons of Korah were spared (Numbers 26:10–11). While Korah didn't care about the presence of God, one of his far-off grandsons, the man who wrote this psalm, longed for God's presence and wanted to be near him. What about you? Do you long to be near God? Our sinful hearts want to turn us away from God, but God is always calling and drawing us to come and worship him. Pray and listen. Can you hear the voice of God calling to you to believe?

The author of this psalm used the picture of a thirsty deer to describe his longing to worship God in Jerusalem at the temple where he knows God's presence lives. The son (or sons) of Korah who wrote this psalm is away from Jerusalem, but he longs to return and worship God (v. 2). Think about how different the Sons of Korah who wrote this Psalm are from their great far-off Grandfather Korah who rebelled against Moses. Even though what Korah did was very wrong, God still had mercy for his sons. Now anytime we feel like God is far from us, we can pray this wonderful psalm and allow the words to comfort us.

Psalm 43

KEY IDEA:

Look for the story hidden in the psalm.

QUESTION TO ANSWER:

What story is Psalm 43 telling us?

Like so many psalms, Psalm 42 tells a story. The man described in this song longs to worship God in Jerusalem (the holy hill of Psalm 43:3) at the temple (tabernacle, altar). For some reason, he is living in the land of Jordan (42:6) far from the temple in Jerusalem, and he is unable to go home. The ungodly people around him are making fun of his longing for God. (Sounds a lot like Psalm 42!) They mock (make fun of) and taunt him saying, "Where is your God?" (42:3, 10). But the man in the story does not give up. He rejects their mocking. Again, and again he speaks words of faith to his weary soul saying, "Why are you downcast, O my soul? Hope in God for I shall yet praise him." These hope-filled words are repeated in the chorus both psalms share (verses 42:5, 11; 43:5).

Psalm 42 and 43 seem to go together to form one song. Notice how the chorus from Psalm 42:5 and 11 repeats in Psalm 43:5. Psalm 43 doesn't say it is written by the sons of Korah, but it is grouped with their psalms. Since it shares the same chorus as Psalm 42, and seems to continue Psalm 42, the editor placed it with the other Korah psalms.

Today, we can take courage from this psalm writer's example. There are times in our lives when others will tempt us to do the wrong thing. If we say "no" to joining them, because we want to follow God, they may mock us too. But we can take courage from the example of the sons of Korah and stand with God against those who reject him. If anyone makes fun of us for praising God or obeying God's Word, we can come look at Psalms 42 and 43 and find comfort and say to our weary soul as we pray, "Hope in God!"

Psalm 50

KEY IDEA:

Try and figure out who or what a psalm is about.

QUESTION TO ANSWER:

What clue tells us Psalm 50 is God speaking to us?

When God wanted to speak to his people, he delivered the message through a prophet like Jeremiah, Isaiah, and Elijah. God shared his message with the prophet who would then speak it to the people. Sometimes prophets were called seers because God gave them prophetic visions to share with his people. A few of the prophets, like David, Asaph, and Heman, were musical prophets; they passed on God's message through the words of their songs.

King David chose Asaph and his sons to lead worship in the house of the Lord (1 Chronicles 25:6) and prophecy through song (1 Chronicles 16:7; 25:1). Long after David and Asaph died, their prophetic songs lived on, and we have them preserved in the book of Psalms. Later, when quoting one of Asaph's psalms, Matthew called him a prophet (Matthew 13:35).

Psalm 50 is one of Asaph's prophetic psalms. Notice how in verse 7 Asaph speaks for God. Asaph writes, "Hear O Israel and I will speak . . . I am God, your God." Asaph wasn't saying he was God, he was repeating God's words to Israel.

Asaph's prophecy from Psalm 50 shares a simple message: God didn't want Israel to sacrifice because it was the law. God wanted them to sacrifice because they loved him and were thankful for all he did for them. God was ready to help them in their day of trouble and wanted Israel to love and depend on him.

So, what about us? Do we go to church because it is the right thing to do, or do we go because we love God? Do we serve others so they will like us? Do we sing loud or lift our hands for other people to see or because we love God? Just like Israel, God wants us to lift our voices to praise him because we are thankful for all he has done for us and love him in our hearts. God offers to help us in our time of need.

Psalm 52

Look for clues in the superscripts.

What do we learn from the superscript from Psalm 52?

A superscript is the short description written at the beginning of a psalm. Look up Psalm 52 and you will see a short description about a man named Doeg the Edomite. The superscript often gives us a clue to which Bible story the psalm is connected to.

Psalm 52 is a song of judgment against a man named Doeg the Edomite. Here is how the story goes. King Saul was angry with David and planned to kill him (1 Samuel 20:32–33). As a result, David fled and met Ahimelech the priest and asked him for food and a sword. Ahimelech gave David bread to eat and Goliath's sword and kept David's whereabouts a secret. But one of Saul's herdsman, Doeg the Edomite, saw Ahimelech help David. Doeg betrayed David by reporting what he saw back to King Saul. King Saul sent for Ahimelech, his family, and the other priests. Ahimelech stood up for David admitting he helped him. Then Saul became very angry and ordered his guard to kill the priests, but the guard would not strike down God's holy men. So King Saul ordered Doeg to kill them. Doeg the Edomite obeyed and killed them all along with their wives, children, and livestock.

One of the priests escaped and fled to David and told him what had happened. When David heard he said, "That day, when Doeg the Edomite was there, I knew he would be sure to tell Saul. I am responsible for the death of your whole family" (1 Samuel 22:22 NIV).

Psalm 52 speaks judgment against Doeg for his wicked sins. David declares that God will one day pluck Doeg out of his tent and destroy him (Psalm 52:5). The people of God will see God's judgment and fear the Lord, but laugh at Doeg as God repays him for his evil deeds (Psalm 52:6). Rather than get angry and seek his own revenge, David placed his trust in the lovingkindness of God and looked to God to judge Doeg for his evil deeds.

We can be sure God answered David's prayer for justice. Today, looking back on this story, we can learn from Doeg's sins. He trusted in riches instead of God (Psalm 52:7) and loved evil more than good (Psalm 52:3). In the end, bad guys never win. If ever someone wrongs us, we should not seek revenge, but trust God to avenge wrongs done against us.

Psalm 72

KEY IDEA:
Try and figure out who or what a psalm is about.

QUESTION TO ANSWER:
Who is Psalm 72 about?

The very first line of Psalm 72 says, "of Solomon," but when we come to the last line of the psalm we read, "The prayers of David, the son of Jesse, are ended." So is this a psalm written by Solomon, or a prayer offered by his father King David? Some Bible scholars think it may be both. Imagine an elderly King David lying in bed, with his son Solomon at his side. David is speaking the word of Psalm 72 over his son. Solomon records every word, so he won't forget.

King David's prophetic prayer over his son came true in Solomon's lifetime. Solomon ruled all the land (v. 8 and see 1 Kings 4:21) and the kings of the desert came to bow down to him (v. 9). Kings brought Solomon gold (v. 15). In fact, each year kings gave Solomon fifty thousand pounds of gold and the queen of Sheba herself brought him tribute (1 Kings 10:13–15). People came to Solomon in distress (v. 12) and Solomon helped them (1 Kings 3:16–28).

We see hints of a third king in this psalm—King Jesus. Only in Jesus will all the nations be blessed and all will call him blessed (v. 17). While the nations praised Solomon during his rule, it is at the name of Jesus that every knee will one day bow (Philippians 2:10). David ends his prayer by praising God as the one who is blessed, "who alone does wondrous things" (v. 18).

One day, when King Jesus returns to judge the heavens and the earth the words of Psalm 72:19 will be fulfilled. All sin and evil will be defeated and all the peoples of the earth will praise him (Revelation 7:9) and the whole earth will be filled with his glory.

> After this I heard what seemed to be the loud voice of a great multitude in heaven, crying out, "Hallelujah! Salvation and glory and power belong to our God."
> (Revelation 19:1)

The question for each of us is will we be numbered with the people who are filled with joy at the return of Jesus because they believe? Or will we be numbered with the people who are filled with fear because they refused to believe and will be judged?

Psalm 73

KEY IDEA:

Learn from the psalm writer's emotion.

QUESTION TO ANSWER:

How would you describe Asaph's passion for God from this psalm?

Psalm 73 shows us Asaph's passion and heart for God. Even though Asaph experiences hard times, his love for God keeps him from falling away. Psalm 73 begins with a confession. Asaph confesses he nearly turned away from following God. Earlier in verse 3 of the psalm, Asaph tells us he got upset when he saw people were sinning against God, but everything was going well for them. Asaph was tempted to speak out against God in anger and frustration, but he caught himself. Instead of turning away from God, Asaph turned toward him. He went to the temple to ask God why those who did evil deeds were being blessed. It was there in the temple that God showed Asaph the wicked will be judged by God in the end. Nobody gets away with their sin (Psalm 73:27).

We see Asaph's passion for God from his prayer in verses 25 and 26:

"Whom have I in heaven but you? And there is nothing on earth that I desire besides you. My flesh and my heart may fail, but God is the strength of my heart and my portion forever."

Asaph loved two things above all else. First, Asaph loved the Lord. Second, Asaph loved to retell the deeds of the Lord to his children and grandchildren. He wanted the next generation to know and worship the God he loved. Asaph knew if he turned against God, his bad example would ruin his ability to tell the next generation and call them to love God (v. 15). But because he made the Lord God his refuge he could tell of God's wondrous works (v. 28). Asaph's prayer in verses 25 and 26 is a prayer we should all memorize and is an example to follow as we one day share the good news of Jesus with our children.

Psalm 74

KEY IDEA:

Scholars are not certain all the authors listed in the superscripts wrote the psalms attributed to them.

QUESTION TO ANSWER:

Did Asaph or someone else write Psalm 74?

While Psalm 74 bears Asaph's name, many Bible teachers think someone else may have written it because the psalm describes events that took place long after Asaph died. The first eleven verses of Psalm 74 tell the story of the ransacking and looting of the temple of God in Jerusalem. Since the destruction of the temple was more than four hundred years after Asaph was born, Asaph most certainly died by the time of the invasion of Babylon.

Bible teachers believe this psalm describes the account of King Jehoiachin's (Jay-hoy-a-chin) surrender to King Nebuchadnezzar (2 Kings 24:8–17). Jehoiachin was eighteen years old when he became king of Jerusalem. He did not obey God but followed the evil ways of his father. Therefore, God sent the armies of Babylon to surround his city and cut off all of their supplies. Rather than turn away from his sin and call out to the Lord, the young king surrendered his family and the city to the enemy. The King of Babylon took him prisoner and carried off the treasures of Jerusalem, including the gold lamp stand and other temple articles. Then the army of Babylon cut the other temple items up into pieces (2 Kings 24:13).

Psalm 74 is either a prophecy written by Asaph that describes future events or a record of history looking back, written by someone else. Some scholars believe Psalm 74 was written by someone else and is only dedicated to Asaph. Either way, it does not change what we can learn from this psalm. The psalm writer believes God is all-powerful and cries out to God to remember his people (v. 2). The second half of the psalm (vv. 12–23) recounts the powerful deeds of the Lord and asks God to "rise up and defend" his people (Psalm 74:22). Whenever we are in trouble, we can pray the same prayer and ask God to come to our aid. We never have to give in to discouragement or unbelief. God is all-powerful and will deliver us.

Psalm 77

Notice how the psalm writers share their struggles in their prayers.

What are Asaph's struggles and how does he find help in God?

One of the most encouraging aspects of the Psalms is how the authors honestly share their struggles. Asaph opens Psalm 77 with an honest account of his trials. In verse 2 he tells us he is in a "day of my trouble," and he is trying to "seek the Lord." But then he gives us this honest report: "my soul refuses to be comforted." He says that whenever he remembers a truth about God could help him, he moans and faints (v. 3). Asaph says he is "so troubled that he cannot speak" (v. 4).

Have you ever felt like Asaph? Perhaps you are going through a difficult trial and someone gives you a Bible verse like, "Trust in the LORD with all your heart and lean not on your own understanding; in all your ways submit to him, and he will make your paths straight" (Proverbs 3:5–6 NIV). Perhaps you think to yourself, *That is easy to say, but it is not helping me right now.* That is how Asaph felt.

Isn't it good to see the struggles of some of our Bible heroes up close and personal in the Psalms? David prayed in Psalm 13:1, "How long, O LORD? Will you forget me forever?" Have you ever felt like God has forgotten you?

The good news is that those who wrote the Psalms didn't give up on God. We often see how truth helped them in the end. Asaph doesn't give up on God. In spite of his troubles, he refuses to forget God. He tries his best to remember all that God has done (v. 12). Just like Asaph, if we remember how God has delivered his people in the past, we can be encouraged and strengthened in our trials.

Psalm 78

Compare psalms by the same author to see what you can learn.

What can we learn about Asaph from his psalms?

You could call Psalm 78 Asaph's theme song. We first saw Asaph write about sharing God's deeds with the next generation in Psalm 73:28. Here in Psalm 78, Asaph charges us to "tell the next generation the praiseworthy deeds of the LORD, his power, and the wonders he has done" (v. 4 NIV). Asaph's hope was that the next generation would put their trust in God (v. 7). That is why parents read and teach the Bible to their kids. The goal is for you to grow up, and one day when you have kids of your own, pass the truth about God on to your kids— "even the children yet to be born" (v. 6). Then those grandchildren can tell their children—the great grandchildren.

The apostle Matthew quoted Psalm 78, "I will open my mouth in parables, I will utter things hidden since the creation of the world" (Matthew 13:35 NIV). He explained that this verse pointed forward to Jesus's teaching with parables. We know from reading the Gospels that Jesus used parables in his teaching. He told many parables that spoke about his mission and his kingdom—like the man who discovered a treasure in a field (Matthew 13:44) or the merchant who searched for one precious pearl (Matthew 13:45). Looking back today we know Jesus was talking about himself in those short stories. Jesus is both the precious pearl and the hidden treasure. Through these stories Jesus revealed he was the Messiah God promised to send to deliver his people (Matthew 16:20).

When parents teach their children (the next generation) about Jesus, they are following in Asaph's footsteps. Sending Jesus to die for our sins and rise again in victory is the greatest wonder God has ever done.

Psalm 89

KEY IDEA:
Look for themes in the Psalms that are found in both the Old and New Testaments.

QUESTION TO ANSWER:
What theme from Psalm 89 is found in both the Old and New Testaments?

Psalm 89 is the only psalm written by Ethan the Ezrahite. Ethan lived in the days of King David and Solomon. He was a wise man and is compared to Solomon in 1 Kings (1 Kings 4:31). Ethan came from the tribe of Levi and had four brothers (1 Chronicles 2:6), one of which was Heman, a chief musician in David's court.

In the opening four verses of Ethan's psalm, he recounts the promise God gave David to raise up a son after him and establish his throne forever (2 Samuel 7:13). We see this theme in both the Old and New Testaments.

When he spoke to Mary, the angel Gabriel announced Jesus would fulfill God's promise to David. Gabriel said, "You will conceive in your womb and bear a son, and you shall call his name Jesus. He will be great and will be called the Son of the Most High. And the Lord God will give to him the throne of his father David, and he will reign over the house of Jacob forever, and of his kingdom there will be no end" (Luke 1:31–33).

Later in the psalm, in verse 36, Ethan tells us Solomon's offspring "shall endure forever," repeating the promise God first gave his father David. But God's promise, as recounted in this psalm, is bigger than David or Solomon; God's promise points us all the way to Jesus.

We know from Israel's history that in spite of his wisdom, Solomon turned away from the Lord (1 Kings 11:9). Shortly after assuming the throne, Solomon's son, Rehoboam, was not a wise king, and under his rule the kingdom split into two (1 Kings 12). Most of the kings that followed were evil and did not worship the Lord. Even this psalm ends with Ethan asking God: "Lord, where is your steadfast love of old, which by your faithfulness you swore to David?" (Psalm 89:49). The answer Ethan is looking for can only be found in Jesus. Jesus is the offspring of David who sits on an everlasting throne (v. 4).

Psalm 90

KEY IDEA:
Keep the history from the author's life in mind as you read his psalms.

QUESTION TO ANSWER:
What events from Moses's life influence what he wrote in this psalm?

God used Moses to deliver his people from slavery in Egypt. In this psalm, Moses is reflecting on his life and all God has done for him. In delivering his people from the hand of Pharaoh, God brought plagues like frogs, fiery hail, and flies to convince Pharaoh to let God's people go. Then God opened up the Red Sea to allow them to escape Egypt's army (Exodus 14). Even so, the people soon forgot all that God had done to save them and complained about not having enough water and food and made an idol. Instead of rejoicing in all God had done, the people complained.

Whenever we are in trouble, we can remember how God delivered Israel from Egypt. Even when we can't see any way out, we can pray to God, for if he can open up the Red Sea, he can deliver us from our troubles too. When we are going through a long trial that doesn't end we can pray the same prayers Moses prayed, that God would teach us to number our days and give us wisdom (v. 12). Each morning when we wake, even if our trial has not gone away, we can pray and ask God to help us remember his steadfast love so we can be glad (v. 14). This psalm teaches us that we don't need to wait until our trial is over to find joy and delight in God and be glad all our days (v. 15).

Moses lived more than four hundred years before King David wrote his first psalm. That makes Psalm 90, "A Prayer of Moses," the oldest psalm in the Bible. The words of this ancient song remind us important truths about God. He created the earth (v. 2) and he is eternal ("from everlasting to everlasting you are God" v. 2). God rules over man and decides how long he should live and when each man will die and return to the dust (v. 3). God is bigger than time—a thousand years are like a day to God (v. 4). Moses learned that when we see how great God is, it makes all our troubles seem small and helps us see that God can help us in any trial, no matter how big.

Psalm 91

Look for the one key word in a Psalm that tells you what it is about.

What one key word does this psalm teach us?

The message of Psalm 91 can be found in the key word "refuge." A refuge is a safe place to hide for protection, like a shelter from a storm. The message of Psalm 91 is that if we place our trust in God he will save us. God is faithful to his promises. God sent his Son Jesus to die for our sins. He lived a perfect life for us, and died so anyone who trusts in him can be forgiven. Jesus knew and trusted in the promises of Psalm 91, and so can we.

When the devil tempted Jesus in the wilderness, he quoted from Psalm 91:11–12. Satan took Jesus to the top of the temple and challenged him to throw himself down. By quoting these verses Satan was saying something like this, "Go ahead, I dare you to throw yourself down from the temple to test and see if the words of Psalm 91 are true." It is interesting that Satan didn't quote verse 13, which tells us that one day Israel will trample the serpent. Jesus defeated Satan by giving up his life upon the cross to end the curse and provide a way for us to be forgiven.

Jesus did not fall for the devil's dare. He trusted his Father and the words of this psalm, but refused to obey a command from Satan. Jesus knew the promise in verse 13 that he would defeat Satan by the cross and so crush the head of the serpent. So he didn't fall for the devil's trap. After one more temptation, Jesus commanded Satan to "be gone." As soon as Satan fled, angels came to Jesus and comforted him (Matthew 4:10–11). When we trust in Jesus, he sends his Holy Spirit to live inside of us to comfort us in our troubles and to help us say "no" to sin and live for God.

Psalm 100

KEY IDEA:

Look for themes in groupings of psalms.

QUESTION TO ANSWER:

How does Psalm 100 connect to the seven psalms that come before it?

Once you've read through Psalms 93–99, you should be ready to make a joyful noise (Psalm 100:1). Psalm 100 caps off the celebration of God as King by calling us to shout and praise. Go back and skim Psalms 93–99. What do they teach us about the rule of our God and King? Here are a few things we discover:

Our King reigns in majesty (Psalm 93:1).
Our King rules as judge over the earth (Psalm 94:2).
Our King is a God above all gods (Psalm 95:3).
Our King is great (Psalm 96:4).
Our King is righteous and faithful (Psalm 97:2).
Our King brings salvation (Psalm 98:3).
Our King is holy (Psalm 99:5).

Back in Israel's day, King Solomon built a temple in the city of Jerusalem. When the temple was completed, the glory of the Lord came down from heaven and filled the temple with God's presence (2 Chronicles 7:1). When the people saw the glory of God fill the temple, they bowed down. From then on, people traveled to Jerusalem because they knew God reigned over Jerusalem as King, and his presence was in the inner court of the temple. They could see the glory of the Lord, which reminded them of his power and might, but it also reminded them God was with them. The gates and courts of verse 4 of Psalm 100 are the gates of Jerusalem and the court of the temple where God lived.

Jesus predicted the temple building would be destroyed (Mark 13:2), but he promised to send his Spirit to live inside all those who believe (John 14:15–31). So, God's people are the new temple of God. God is with us just as he was with Israel. The God that is described as holy, righteous, faithful, lives within every Christian! That is why we raise our hands and shout and sing! He is with us! He is our King!

Psalm 101

KEY IDEA:
Learn how to apply a psalm to your own life.

QUESTION TO ANSWER:
How can we make David's pledge our prayer and apply Psalm 101 to our lives?

A pledge is a promise. Psalm 101 is King David's pledge to follow God's law and his ways. David promises to live for God (vv. 1–4) and to judge sin in others (vv. 5–8). David also knows he needs God to help him and so he calls out to God, "When will you come to me?" (v. 2).

All of us are called to live for God and guard our lives against sin. We can make David's pledge our prayer. Look through the verses. Which of these lines do you think the Holy Spirit wants you to make as a promise to God? One of the most helpful promises is found in verse 3, "I will not set before my eyes anything that is worthless." David knew the dangers and temptations, which come when we allow ourselves to view sinful images.

If David had to be careful in a day before computers and other screen devices, how much more important is it for us? We should make David's pledge our promise, "I will not set before my eyes anything that is worthless." Whenever we see inappropriate images or messages on our screens we should turn away and tell our parents. Too much screen time can be worthless too. It is easy to forget how long you are playing a game. You can waste hours with nothing to show for your efforts.

David didn't just guard his eyes, he wanted to avoid all evil and he wanted the people of Israel to follow his example. Today, we can take a close look at our lives and turn away from lying, stealing, anger, disrespect of parents, and other sins that take our focus away from God.

Psalm 103

KEY IDEA:

Look for gospel themes in a psalm.

QUESTION TO ANSWER:

Where do you see the gospel foreshadowed in Psalm 103?

The Monte Rosa is the name of the tallest of the snow-capped Swiss Alp mountains. The great pastor Charles Spurgeon compared Psalm 103 to the Monte Rosa. In his seven-book series on the book of Psalms, he said if the psalms were mountains, Psalm 103 would "overtop the rest." He went on to say it is as "the apple tree among the trees of the wood" and "there is too much in the psalm for a thousand pens to write."[1] Spurgeon believed the whole message of the Bible was squeezed into this one psalm.

Gospel words that point to Jesus popped off the page when Charles Spurgeon looked at Psalm 103. Even though David didn't know all the details of God's plan to send Jesus to die on the cross, he believed the essentials of the gospel. David understood only God could forgive his sins (*iniquity* is another word for sin, see v. 3). Only God could redeem his life from the pit (v. 4). "Redeem" is a word that means "buy back." God redeemed us by giving up his only Son Jesus. You see, we are all sold as slaves to sin by the bad things we do and so we all deserve eternal punishment. Jesus redeemed us (bought us back) by dying on the cross and paying the penalty we deserve. Now all those who trust in Jesus are redeemed by his blood (Ephesians 1:7). So, when David tells us God redeems our life from the pit, he is pointing to Jesus.

The best part of this psalm is reading about God's forgiveness. When God removes our sin, he puts them as far away as the east is from the west (v. 12). That means God removes them forever. Those who turn from their sin to trust in Jesus will never face God's wrath for the bad things they have done. The only right response to God's loving forgiveness is to "Bless the LORD," which David repeats seven times in this song. We bless the Lord when we pray like this: *Dear God, thank you for forgiving my sins and crowning me with your love and mercy*.

---

[1]Charles Spurgeon, *Treasury of David*, Volume Two (Peabody, MA: Hendrickson Publishers, 2008), 275.

Psalm 107

KEY IDEA:
Study key phrases you discover in a psalm.

QUESTION TO ANSWER:
Where else have we heard the words east, west, north, and south?

You can do a search on the internet for key words and phrases in the Bible to discover the other places those same words show up. If we do that for "east, west, north, and south," this is some of what we discover.

The opening of Psalm 107 matches a prophesy Isaiah gave. Isaiah wrote, "Fear not, for I am with you; I will bring your offspring from the east, and from the west I will gather you. I will say to the north, Give up, and to the south, Do not withhold; bring my sons from afar and my daughters from the end of the earth, everyone who is called by my name, whom I created for my glory, whom I formed and made" (Isaiah 43:5–7).

Psalm 107 calls for people from all corners of the world—the east, west, north, and south—to declare his salvation. Then the psalm goes on to tell the story of four different groups of people and how God saved them in spite of their sin and foolishness. The author shares the story of God's deliverance of those in prison (vv. 10–16), those who wandered in the desert (Psalm 107:6–9), those who became fools (Psalm 107:17–22) and sailors who God delivered from the storm (Psalm 107:23–32). Psalm 107 ends with a warning to all who read it: "Whoever is wise, let him attend to these things; let them consider the steadfast love of the Lord" (v. 43).

Jesus repeated the promise of Psalm 107 and Isaiah 43: "people will come from east and west, and from north and south, and recline at table in the kingdom of God," (Luke 13:29). God is still gathering his lost children from the four corners of the world today. Do you hear him calling you?

Psalm 109

KEY IDEA:
Learn about the imprecatory psalms.

QUESTION TO ANSWER:
What is an imprecatory psalm?

The word *imprecatory* sounds just like it is written when you break it down into smaller pieces: im-pre-ca-to-ry. *Imprecatory* is a long word used to describe psalms that cry out to God to bring bad consequences upon evil enemies. Psalm 109 is one of the harshest examples of this kind of prayer. David prays that God would appoint a wicked man against his enemy (v. 6), have the bankers (creditor) take all his possessions (v. 11), have strangers steal the fruits and vegetables out of his garden (v. 11), and that God would take his life (v. 9) and leave his children poor, with no inheritance (v. 10) and without anyone to have pity on them (v. 12).

What are we to think of such a prayer? Are we to pray against our enemies? When we think about these psalms, it's important to remember David is asking God to be the judge. It's also important to see how David responded to his enemies. They have attacked David without cause (v. 3); that means David did nothing to hurt them. David did not fight back; he loved his enemies and prayed for them (v. 4). Still they came against him and rewarded his good will with evil and hatred for his love (v. 5).

The Bible tells us never to seek revenge for the evil people do to us, but we are to leave that to God who promises to repay evil with judgment (Romans 12:19). But we can call out to God to defend us from our enemies and to bring justice to them. There is no indication David stopped loving his enemy in this psalm. Psalm 109 gives us a window into how David cries out to God to do what God promises—to deliver us from our enemies. We should also never forget that apart from God's grace, all of us deserve God's judgment. We are all God's enemies and yet he loved us and sent his Son to die for us. That shows us how God treats his enemies and today, after Jesus's death and resurrection, God calls us to share the good news of the gospel even with our enemies.

Psalm 110

Look for verses in the Psalms that are quoted in the New Testament.

What verses of Psalm 110 are quoted in the New Testament?

If you get a study Bible, you can see in the middle reference column all the places a verse is quoted in the rest of the Bible. It is helpful to take note of the times a verse from a psalm is quoted in the New Testament. The New Testament authors often help us understand the meaning of the Old Testament passages they quote.

The Holy Spirit led the New Testament authors to quote Psalm 110 more than any other Old Testament passage. Psalm 110 points forward to the promised deliverer so clearly that the Jews of Jesus's day also believed it was a prophecy of the coming Messiah. So how could David write so clearly about Jesus hundreds of years before he was born? Jesus gives us the answer in Matthew 22:43. King David wrote with the help of the Holy Spirit.

Psalm 110 tells us the Messiah will be the King of Israel (Zion in v. 2) and will be more powerful than all the kings of the earth (v. 5). He will also serve as a priest before God forever, which means he will live forever (v. 4). The writer of Hebrews quotes Psalm 110 and explains that Jesus is the priest David talked about in verse 4 (Hebrews 7:21–24). Jesus gave up his life for us and then after he rose from the dead, Jesus returned to heaven where he began his work as the great High Priest. Jesus stands before the Father and prays for us (Hebrews 7:25–28). The scars on his hands and feet prove before God the payment for our sin was paid for in full.

One of the reasons God gave us prophetic psalms like Psalm 110 is to help us believe and put our trust in God's saving plan through Jesus. So here is the question we should consider: Do I believe and trust in Jesus as my Messiah (the one God sent to die in my place for my sins to rescue me)?

Psalm 127

Look for metaphors (a word picture that teaches us something) in the Psalms and consider what they are teaching.

What are the metaphors of Psalm 127 and what are they trying to teach us?

The Psalms are full of word pictures. For example, Psalm 84:11 says, "For the LORD God is a sun and shield." That doesn't mean God is literally a sun or a shield. Just as the sun is the source of all light and therefore brings life to the earth, so God is our source of life. Just as a shield protects a warrior in battle, so the Lord protects us. So metaphors or word pictures can communicate deep truths in a simple picture.

Psalm 127 uses the metaphor of a builder and a watchman to help us understand why we need God's help. Every builder knows how hard it is to build a house alone, without an extra set of hands to help. In the same way, one watchman cannot guard the whole city by himself. No matter which way he faces, the enemy can always attack to his rear. The same is true for us today.

Solomon wrote this psalm to teach the people of Israel that they needed God. Without God's help they never could have conquered their enemies.

Without God's help they could not have built the temple, nor could they defend their city. So all the glory of their beautiful temple and city belonged to God. Sadly the people didn't remember Solomon's words and turned away from the Lord to worship idols. That is when God disciplined them by allowing the destruction of the temple.

Today God is building his church, joining people together as "living stones" (1 Peter 2:4–5). And we still need God's help to save us and change our hard hearts. We also need God to help us day-to-day in things like choosing to trust him instead of worry, and choosing to love others instead of giving into anger. Parents can teach their children about God, but only God can touch a child's heart and open their eyes to believe and add another living stone to the building. We can do nothing without God (John 15:4). The good news is God is ready to help us. All we have to do is ask and depend on him.

Psalm 150

KEY IDEA:
Always pay attention to the ending of a book.

QUESTION TO ANSWER:
What does the last psalm teach us about the entire book of Psalms?

You could sum up the message of Psalm 150 with one short phrase: break out the instruments and praise! But here is the question: What are we celebrating? While this last psalm doesn't give us a long answer, it gives us two reasons to praise in verse 2. Praise God for his excellent greatness and praise God for his mighty works. If this were the first psalm in the book of Psalms a person might read it and think, *What's the big deal? I don't feel like getting excited*. But when you read this psalm last, after all you learn through the Psalms, you have many reasons to dance and sing.

Let's review some of those reasons. God is great, for he is the one who created the whole world and everything you see for us to enjoy (Psalms 8:3; 19:1; 24:2; 139:13; 146:6). God's most special "mighty deed" is his work of salvation (Psalm 150:2). Even though all people have sinned against God and deserve to be punished, God did not turn away from us and judge us (Psalms 14, 36, and 51). For God is slow to anger and abounding in steadfast love (Psalms 86:5; 103:8; 145:8). Because of this, God saved us instead by sending his Son (Psalm 2:7) to be nailed to a cross in our place (Psalm 22:16) and be rejected by God the Father (Psalm 22:1). But because Jesus had no sin, the grave could not hold him and he rose again (Psalm 16:10). Now all who trust in God will be saved (Psalm 118:14–24).

So now you know the book of Psalms is all about Jesus and the wonderful way he saves us from our sin, join the celebration of Psalm 150. Find an instrument, any instrument. Grab a wooden spoon and saucepan and bang them loud with all your might. Dance and jump; shout and sing. God's promised salvation has come and all those who trust in the Lord will be saved. So, "sing praises to God, sing praises! Sing praises to our King, sing praises!" (Psalm 47:6).

You can join in the praise right now. One of our most loved hymns is called "The Doxology" and was written by Thomas Ken in 1674, but it is still widely sung today. This hymn can help you answer the final call of the book of Psalms, "Let everything that has breath praise the Lord!"

> "Praise God from whom all blessings flow;
> Praise him, all creatures here below;
> Praise him above, ye heavenly host;
> Praise Father, Son, and Holy Ghost. Amen"

> Tomas Ken, 1674

Acknowledgments

I would like to thank the many scholars whose books formed the foundation for my writing of this book. I am particularly indebted to O. Palmer Robertson, whose book *The Flow of the Psalms* provided the key framework I followed in understanding the larger structure and organization of the Psalms. I commend his work to anyone interested in further study. For those of you familiar with his writing, you will see his fingerprints on the pages of *WonderFull*. I would also like to give credit to Charles Spurgeon and his multivolume commentary *The Treasury of David*, as well as Patrick Henry Reardon's *Christ in the Psalms*. Tremper Longman III and his book *How to Read the Psalms* and Richard Belcher Jr.'s book *The Messiah and the Psalms* gave me the confidence to search for Christ in each psalm. Beyond these authors, I'd like to thank the pastors and staff of Covenant Fellowship for their ongoing support and encouragement. I am also indebted to Bob Kauflin, Ken Mellinger, Jim Donohue, Barbara Juliani, Matt Searls, Nancy Winter, Ruth Castle, and Jocelyn Flenders, all of whom read through various drafts and offered helpful critique. I am most grateful to my wife, Lois, who gladly listened to each morning's writing as I worked my way through the Psalms sharing my discoveries, often through tears.